MAKE STRESS WORK FOR YOU

GW00597382

MAKE STRESS WORK FOR YOU

Helen Graham

GILL & MACMILLAN

Gill & Macmillan Ltd
Goldenbridge
Dublin 8
with associated companies throughout the world
© Helen Graham 1997
0 7171 2598 X
Index compiled by
Stephanie Dagg

Design and print origination by
O'K Graphic Design, Dublin

Printed by
ColourBooks Ltd, Dublin

All rights reserved. No part of this publication may be copied,
reproduced or transmitted in any form or by any means, without
permission of the publishers.

A catalogue record is available for this book from the British Library.

1 3 5 4 2

CONTENTS

INTRODUCTION

Although a connection between adverse life events and serious illness has been recognised since ancient times, the concept of stress was not clearly formulated until the 1920s. It was established subsequently that prolonged stress does have physiological effects, which include suppression of the immune system. These effects provide clear-cut evidence for a direct link between psychological events (mind) and physical processes (body) — a link formerly denied within orthodox Western medicine.

Stress is now recognised as contributing to 75 per cent of all illnesses, and in recent years it has become fashionable to think of stress itself as the major disease of the twentieth century. Accordingly stress has become a negative concept and stress avoidance has become the goal of many people pursuing health and happiness.

However, it is now known that the interaction between life events and the individual is considerably more complex than was first believed and that the total avoidance of stress may be undesirable and unhealthy. As in most things, balance is required, and to achieve this balance we need to know how to identify not only the aspects of our life that cause us too much stress, but also when we need to seek stimulation.

This book explains the need for balance and how it can be achieved by way of simple self-awareness exercises. These exercises are based upon ones I have developed in the courses and workshops on the psychology of health and healing that I have held for many years. By way of illustration, I have also included the experiences and observations of the participants in these workshops, as well as comment from individuals in one-to-one therapy. (The names used here have, for the most part, been changed throughout.)

The word *stress* is thought to derive from the Latin *stringere*, meaning 'to pull tight', which accurately describes some of the major effects of stress on the body. This idea is conveyed in everyday phrases people use to describe the experience of stress, such as 'being uptight', 'strung out' or 'strung up'. These phrases also have connotations of being out of control. By contrast, the phrase 'to pull strings' means to exert power or influence, usually in a way that is hidden or unobtrusive.

The purpose of this book is to help you to learn how to take control of yourself and your life — to pull your *own* strings — and to use stress positively, to your advantage, making it work *for* you, not against you. It sets out and explains the steps you can take to identify the sources and effects of stress in your life, how you can eliminate unnecessary tensions and relieve unavoidable stress.

Chapter One explains how stress produces tension and low levels of energy. It includes a simple exercise to help you assess your energy level and the ways in which you lose energy. (A more detailed energy questionnaire is provided at the end of the book.) It also identifies the major sources of stress and the issues you need to address in order to relieve it.

Chapter Two explains the way in which you block emotion through muscle tension; how you can identify your emotional blocks and the energies pent-up within them, and the characteristic ways you use to defend yourself against the anxiety they generate. It presents exercises in progressive relaxation, breathing and visualisation to help you unwind and release the mental and physical tensions associated with this stress.

Chapter Three explains the effects of stress on the body and the illnesses that can result. It distinguishes between *stress* (the state of high arousal produced in response to threatening situations) and *stressors* (those events and circumstances you perceive as threatening); includes a visualisation exercise to help you to identify the particular stressors in your life of which you may be unaware; and explains the ways in which visualisation provides beneficial insights into ordinarily hidden aspects of yourself.

Chapter Four examines why stress avoidance may be more harmful than otherwise, and how the brain strives for balance between over- and understimulation. It explains how such techniques as meditation, hypnosis, relaxation, Autogenic Training and visualisation can help you to eliminate stress by achieving a psychological and physical balance; provides instructions on how to meditate, elicit the Relaxation Response and use self-hypnosis for relaxation; and offers a different way of eliminating unnecessary stressors by way of guided imagery.

Chapter Five shows you how to handle the stressors you cannot eliminate, by changing your attitude to and taking responsibility for them. It also shows the importance of changing your attitude towards yourself — the source of much of your stress — and shows you how to do so by expressing, accepting, asserting, valuing, indulging and thinking positively about yourself, managing your time successfully and taking life less seriously.

Chapter Six explains how certain food substances produce a stress-like response, how others exacerbate stress-related illnesses, and how some of the substances in food are affected by stress. It shows you how you can increase your resistance to stress through diet, exercise and bodywork; gives advice and guidance on healthy eating, including a low-stress diet, and on what to eat and drink if you suffer from stress-related diseases; and provides guidelines on beginning a low-stress exercise programme.

Chapter Seven explains how you can identify and handle the stressful energies of other people. It presents exercises in energy sensing; explains how you can relieve energy blocks in others and redistribute and rebalance their energies; and describes how you are susceptible to the influence of other people, and how you yourself can become more influential and effective.

Each chapter concludes with a summary which lists the key points discussed in the chapter. There is an energy questionnaire at the end of the book which is preceded by an inventory of quick tips for immediate stress relief, 'Let Go of Your Hang-Ups'.

RECOGNISING HOW STRUNG UP YOU ARE

I can't explain myself, I'm afraid, because I'm not myself,
you see. Oh, my fur and whiskers. It is this, it is this, that
oppresses my soul.
Lewis Carroll, *Alice in Wonderland*

ENERGY PROBLEMS

Ordinarily we describe ourselves and others in terms of energy, as high or low in energy: 'full' of energy or 'drained' of it. This is also a way in which we customarily assess our health and well-being. For this reason, and because most of us function at less than optimum energy levels much of the time, energy problems are among those most commonly presented to doctors and other healthcare practitioners. Sometimes the problem is excess energy. This is fairly common in children, whereas from childhood onwards energy problems more usually relate to loss of or lack of energy: the feeling that our 'get up and go' has got up and gone.

Doctors typically describe high energy in terms of hyperactivity or mania; and low energy in terms of fatigue and depression; or refer to it in shorthand as ME, TATT and SAD (Myalgic Encephalomyelitis — or chronic fatigue syndrome — Tired All The Time syndrome and Seasonal Affective Disorder respectively). These labels do not explain the problem or help us to deal with it. Unfortunately this is also true of most doctors: they may suggest rest or relaxation, exercise, a tonic, taking vitamins, making dietary changes and such like, but these remedies are invariably ineffective.

Edmund Jacobsen, the doctor who pioneered studies of relaxation during the 1930s, demonstrated that most people generally don't know how to rest or relax. They often don't feel like taking exercise either: well over 50 per cent of all people who take up exercise give up within a few weeks. The reasons they offer for doing so is that they don't have time for exercise and it is inconvenient. Even when exercise is medically prescribed for the treatment of serious illness, few people continue to do so without supervision. Only 6 per cent of patients who have suffered a heart attack continue exercise therapy. Almost half of them report that exercise is inconvenient; 25 per cent dislike exercise; and 30 per cent find it boring.[1] Many people find that changes of diet and vitamin intake don't necessarily increase their energy. Indeed all these remedies can and often do increase the symptoms of energy *loss*.

This is not altogether the fault of doctors, however. The problem lies in the fact that, although we commonly refer to how we feel in terms of energy, few of us have a very clear idea of what energy is. Even within the scientific community there are uncertainties and confusion about the concept of energy. Definitions of the term are at best somewhat vague and have altered significantly over recent decades with changes in our understanding of the functioning of the universe.

ENERGY AS WORK

From the seventeenth century until relatively recently, scientific thinking was based on a view of the universe and everything in it as resembling a vast machine. Within this framework, energy is the work involved in activating the various components of the machine, and applies to all physical bodies and systems, including the human body which is conceived as being operated by various 'drives'. The driving force of the body is the muscles which act, like pistons, to move it and make it 'work', which they achieve by tension or tightening.

Although the scientific model on which it was based is now outmoded, this view of energy as the capacity of a body or system to work remains valid. Few of us would dispute that running up a mountain or digging a trench is hard work. However, most of us are unaware of how much work our muscles routinely undertake. You may not realise, for instance, that you can use more energy lying on a sofa watching television for several hours than if you were digging a trench with a pickaxe. Once the initial impetus is provided, swinging the pickaxe uses relatively little energy because of inertia. By contrast, keeping muscles constantly tense, as many of us do when we are lounging in front of the television or lying in bed, uses considerable energy. Paradoxically, therefore, wielding a pickaxe all day can involve much less work for the body than 'relaxing' in the evening.

Energy as Movement

The contemporary view of energy derives from twentieth-century physicists' understanding of the universe. This view is quite different from the earlier machine model, yet it coincides with ancient thinking about the nature of reality. Indeed the word *energy* originates in the ancient Greek for 'activity', *energeia*. The ancient Greeks believed that the entire universe consists of dynamic patterns of change or movement. Accordingly, every phenomenon within the universe consists of energy and each has a characteristic vibration. Modern physics confirms this view. It is now accepted that colour, sound and light are merely different forms of energy — vibrations of varying rates — as are thoughts, images and emotions, and all material things, and physicists can explain how matter, or mass, and energy are simply different aspects of the same phenomenon. It is this relationship, expressed in Einstein's famous equation $E=mc^2$, which forms the basis of modern physics.

Material objects such as the human body are also energy, or forms of movement. The components of our body vibrate at different rates, and our physical body moves or vibrates at a lower rate than the non-physical aspects, such as our thoughts and feelings. Whereas our physical body is activated by its muscles, they in turn are moved by our feelings or *emotions* — literally 'that which move us' — and the thoughts that motivate us (from the Latin *motio*, 'a moving'). When we act in accordance with our emotions, we express our feelings. Hence this energy can move or progress freely; it can flow.

How We Block Our Energy

We need to control or repress those emotions we do not wish to show or express. We do this by blocking or obstructing the flow of energy through tension — quite literally holding the energy in our muscles rather than releasing it and expressing it through appropriate action. Emotional blocks are therefore also physical restrictions. What is not expressed through the body is expressed within it as tension in certain muscle groups. This 'trapped' or pent-up energy is not realised or acted on; it remains potential energy, and we are unaware that this is so. The result is that we feel drained of energy and yet we don't know why. When this tension is maintained over time, the effort involved may be considerable, progressively draining energy resources, tiring the body and imposing strain or stress upon it. We become 'worn out' although we are unaware of doing anything physically strenuous. Similarly when our thoughts don't find expression — when we don't 'speak our minds' or act upon our motives — we repress these energies. So our mental blocks are also physical blocks, maintained through muscle tension. Whenever we repress our feelings, our energy is drained through muscle tension, even though we are unaware of the effort we are making.

ASSESSING YOUR ENERGY LEVEL

The degree of energy you experience at any time depends on the extent to which you are draining energy through maintaining muscle tension. It is determined by how much or little of yourself you are expressing. You can gain some idea of your current energy level by answering the following questions:

- How would you rate your present energy level on a scale of 0–10?
- How does this compare with your normal energy level?
- How do you think you might be losing energy?

You may find the energy questionnaire at the end of the book helpful in providing a more detailed assessment of your current energy level.

LOW ENERGY

Some people don't like to admit to feeling low in energy because they assume others will score higher. You may be one of these people, in which case ask yourself how often you put yourself down in relation to others, or are concerned about being put down by them. Both these tendencies are likely to lead you not to express yourself fully, to use up energy in achieving this, and to feel tense.

Working with wide-ranging groups in courses and workshops, I have found that many people are greatly relieved to discover that they are not the only ones who feel this way. This reluctance to admit to a low rating often reflects anxiety about low achievement in a society that demands us all to be high achievers. What psychologists term a 'social desirability factor' — the desire to be seen to conform with others —

influences us all to some degree; and this in turn influences what we express of ourselves, how controlled we are and how much of our energy this uses up.

You may not like to admit even to yourself that your energy is low. Most of us want to see ourselves in a positive light, which reflects the extent to which we express what we *believe* we should think and feel, rather than what we *do* think and feel.

You may not like to admit to feeling low in energy because feeling low has connotations of being 'down' or 'depressed'. As we have seen, our energy level also reflects emotional and mental states as well as our physical condition. For some of us, admitting to feeling low, 'down' or depressed is tantamount to admitting failure, because being 'on a high' is yet another of the goals of our achievement-oriented culture, while feeling low suggests that something isn't working in our life.

To admit to feeling low in energy may provoke anxiety about your health and well-being, and concern that your body isn't 'working' properly. When it is working well, the activities we engage in seem easy and natural, effortless, enjoyable and satisfying: they seem to flow, we 'go with the flow'; we are wholly absorbed in them. Such activities engage the whole of us and consequently feel 'wholesome' — conducive to our health and well-being; and they *are*, quite literally, because *health* means 'to be whole' (from the German *heilen* and the Old English *hael*, meaning 'whole'). In short, we feel energetic and alive.

It is quite a different story when our energy level feels low. Our activities seem difficult, an effort, a drag. Rather than flow with them, we find we 'can't get on' with them. We make little or no progress; we tire easily and can't concentrate; we find it difficult to 'stick with' them, and are easily distracted. We may feel unwell, quite 'ill' or 'sick' even at the thought of these activities. We may say that we're 'sick to death' of them; that they are 'killing' us. In fact, as we shall see later (Chapter Three), they often are.

Suzie's experience illustrates this well. She had been studying for three years for an academic qualification. Towards the end of this period she began to feel that her heart was no longer in her studies. What formerly had been interesting to her and easy became a painstaking chore. She told me:

> 'I realised that what I used to complete in one hour now took all day. I just couldn't concentrate. I began to worry that I would fail. Then I'd think, "I'm young; I should be able to cope," but I felt terrible. I am so relieved it's over. I feel that since completing the course my life has been given back to me.'

It seems we all know how much we should be able to achieve without feeling exhausted, but most of us don't realise that anything we attempt is in addition to the workload we habitually impose on ourselves by not expressing ourselves. If in the activities you undertake you express yourself fully, then you do so without tension and with minimal expenditure of energy. Performing these activities seems easy and natural. However, performing certain activities can feel like hard work if they require you to control yourself in the process. Suzie almost 'burned herself out' working at something she had outgrown. She wanted to move on; to be able to express herself in newer interests and pursuits, not to be constrained by the old.

Suzie is young and couldn't understand why she was experiencing difficulty. Many people who feel as Suzie did attribute it to ageing; they consider lack of energy natural because age 'takes it out of you'. If you've ever told yourself or others 'it's my age' or 'time of life' as an excuse for not feeling or performing well, pause to consider whether in fact it is age taking your life away, or you giving it away; by not living it in the sense of truly expressing who and what you are, but rather by expressing what others expect you to.

FLUCTUATING ENERGY

Almost certainly you will have experienced variations in energy levels at different periods of your life, and almost certainly this will correspond to those periods of your life when you failed to express yourself as authentically as you might have done. For this reason people I have worked with in groups often find that their energy level begins to rise almost as soon as they have reported their loss of energy to others. They often say that they feel much better simply for having done so, or that they feel relieved. These feelings are not an illusion: by admitting them, the people concerned have released something of themselves that formerly may not have been expressed, and this necessarily involves some relief of tension.

Healthy young children generally express themselves spontaneously and authentically; they have seemingly boundless energy. If you were a healthy child, you may remember that feeling. More probably you remember the frustration of being sent to bed early when you wanted to continue playing, or having to sit still when you wanted to be on the move. Almost certainly you will remember learning to do as you're told and, as you became older, having to curb your energy so as to avoid being told off or punished in other ways. As an older child and adolescent, you no doubt needed to let off steam, and you may have released pent-up energy through sport, dancing or engaging in other vigorous activity.

Now you probably wonder what happened to all that energy, or wonder at the energy of the young. It isn't that younger people have more energy than you do; rather that they use it differently. They tend to express themselves through action rather than 'contain' themselves by way of muscle tension. As they get older, they too will tend to experience lower levels of energy if, in conforming to the requirements of others, they become more controlled in their self-expression and therefore less spontaneous.

Energy levels may also vary with the time of day, time of

week, time of the month, as well as the time of life. You may find that you feel lower in energy on weekdays than at weekends, or vice versa; on certain days of the week or month. You may find that they vary with different company or when engaged in different activities. If so, it is worth considering at which times, in whose company and during which activities you are able to be yourself.

HIGH ENERGY

Certain activities are often thought of as 'taking it out of you'; as draining your energy. Many of the people I have worked with in groups have said to me, 'You must be absolutely drained after a workshop. Aren't you completely worn out afterwards?' They are very surprised when I tell them that my experience is quite the opposite. I usually feel extremely energised at the end of the day. Unless I use this energy, I remain so high I cannot sleep and so after a long day's work invariably I will spend several hours writing. The reason for this is that by working in groups I am expressing myself. In so doing, I often release energy or aspects of myself that do not find expression in other ways. As my mental and emotional blockages are swept away, ideas, thoughts, feelings, perceptions, impressions and insights flow freely. Writing, which is another means of self-expression, is one way in which I 'go with the flow' of these outpourings. Talking is another. Sometimes I simply feel like dancing. These are merely different ways of transforming this energy, or putting it to work.

Many people experience high energy levels only infrequently because, for reasons we will go on to look at, they are rarely able to express themselves authentically or genuinely. Many actively seek this experience, and when they cannot achieve it through their ordinary activities and pursuits, will try to 'get high' in other ways. Drugs and various stimulants appear to offer a short cut, but all too frequently the much sought-after rush of energy is short-lived and is followed by a disproportionately severe 'low'.

The distinguished professor of psychology Abraham Maslow insisted that the only way in which we can achieve what he termed *peak experiences*, and transcend our ordinary personal experience in the attainment of some ultimate experience or reality, is by fulfilling or actualising all our potentials and giving full expression to ourselves. He perceived this self-actualisation as equivalent to perfect health.[2]

Certainly those people who rate their energy levels as consistently high usually epitomise good health and well-being. They often also have great charisma, personal magnetism, power or forcefulness. Such people are relatively few and far between, though. In any group of people the majority will typically rate their usual energy as ranging from 3–7, with an average of around 4. A few will rate their energy as lower still — as 1 or even nil.

You can test the truth of this assertion by asking your family, friends or colleagues to rate their energy on this ten-point scale. You will find that some of those who rate their energy as consistently very low seem anxious, depressed, drawn, dispirited, harassed, tired, run down or worn out. You may be surprised to find that some of the individuals you think of as high in energy in fact rate themselves as low. You may also find that while you rate yourself as consistently low in energy, others around you see you as highly energetic. In order to understand why this is, we need to consider the third of our initial questions: how do you think you might be losing energy?

ENERGY LOSS

You may find that you have to give more thought to this question than to the others, but in my experience few people have difficulty providing answers, although these may surprise them. Typical responses are as follows:

> 'I find the constant hassles at work/home drain my energy.'

'Other people drain my energy; they always want something.'

'My boss drains my energy by making impossible demands on me.'

'I feel so low in energy every morning, waking up to face a new day with the kids, that I can hardly drag myself out of bed.'

'Running around trying to do too much, trying to fit everything in, wears me out.'

'Constantly being on the go grinds me down.'

'I get really run down by the sheer pressure of work, and depressed by the prospect of it.'

'I lose energy to people all the time by trying to please them.'

'Arguments with my parents/children are wearing.'

'My husband is very difficult. He works hard but does absolutely nothing in and around the home; he expects me to do it all.'

'My partner is a perfectionist. He/she wants everything, including me, to be perfect.'

'Trying to be perfect all the time exhausts me.'

'Worrying about exams and a good career takes up a lot of my energy.'

'Keeping up with others drains me.'

'Simply trying to cope exhausts me.'

'I don't have much energy because I don't exercise enough or eat properly.'

'I drink too much.'

Variations on these themes have been expressed by every group I've worked with. These statements may each appear to be quite different, but if we examine them more closely, it becomes clear that *other people* are considered to be the major drain on our energy. More specifically, it is the *demands* they make on us that take a toll on our energy: their wants, needs, desires, requirements, requests, rules, regulations, instructions and guidelines. In the final analysis, work and examination pressures come down to meeting the demands and requirements of others. Time pressures, timetables, deadlines, appointments and schedules are all requirements imposed by others; as are standards of behaviour, health, beauty and striving for perfection. 'Coping' is about meeting these and all the other demands made upon us. Drinking too much or too often may be an indication that we are not coping very well. Not eating properly or not exercising enough may also be a sign that we have too little time to attend to our own needs.

MEETING YOUR NEEDS

Those people who seem to cope best, who always seem to be on the go and whom we consider to be highly energetic, often rate themselves as having low or no energy. Many of these individuals describe themselves like machines: as 'run down', 'ground down', 'worn out', 'going through the motions', 'driven' by trying to meet the requirements of others. In fact most of us are racing about, chasing about, running around, on the go, trying to keep up with the demands of others, and in the process our own needs are neglected, ignored, not even recognised. We are so preoccupied with dealing with the wants and needs of others that we often don't know that we have needs. Yet each of us has fundamental needs — requirements vital for our own health and well-being — and our basic motives are concerned with meeting these needs.

Abraham Maslow identified two broad classes of needs: *deficiency needs* — extrinsic requirements the individual lacks but which must be provided in order for growth and development to occur; and *growth needs* — which must be met in order for personal development to be achieved. The former include physical needs for air, water, food, shelter and sleep; and emotional needs for safety, security, support, belonging, love, affection, appreciation, esteem, respect and recognition. Growth needs are those which must be fulfilled in order for a person's intrinsic potentials and capabilities to be realised or actualised. These can be considered as spiritual needs in so far as they provide meaning or purpose in life, and are essential to the activating principle or motivation of a person.

Maslow conceived of these needs as organised within a hierarchy (see Figure 1) based upon physical needs, which must be met before psychological needs, which, in turn, must be met before spiritual needs. According to Maslow, each need can only be attended to when a lower one is met, and the more basic it is, the more vital is the necessity to fulfil it. He considered the healthy development of a person as a progression through this hierarchy towards the fulfilment of all needs, or self-actualisation. Health is therefore synonymous with the fulfilment of all personal needs, and illness an indication that important needs are being denied. As such, movement in the direction of autonomy or self-control and away from dependence on others is healthy, as is movement in the direction of self-expression and away from expressing what others want us to.[3]

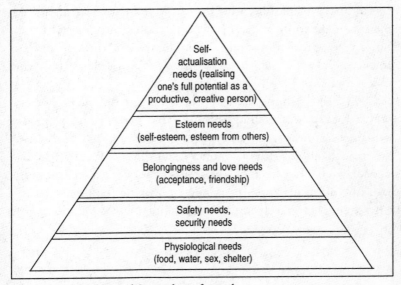

Figure 1: Maslow's hierarchy of needs

For most of us, becoming healthy in all senses of the word, much less remaining so, is rather more difficult to achieve than Maslow's formulation might at first suggest. At birth and for some years afterwards, we are totally dependent on others for the satisfaction of our needs. Clearly if our physical needs for air, water, food, sleep and housing are not met, we are unlikely to thrive, and likely to become ill. Ideally they are met simultaneously within the context of the parent–child relationship; the parents providing the child with love, affection, attention, care, stimulation, contact, touch, security communication in the process of providing for its physical needs.

Fortunately, in most cases, these needs are met, but they are often translated into needs that are more than basic, such as acquiring a certain type of cot, bed or baby carriage, obtaining special foods, or finding living accommodation *with* a garden, and so on. 'Needs' such as these are reinforced and exploited through advertising and the mass media, and a vast industry has grown up around them. The message conveyed is that parents who do not provide appropriately for their offspring (that is, as the industry wants them to) do not love or care for them. As parents want to be seen to be loving and caring, they feel they must feed, dress and equip their children in the appropriate manner, and send them to suitable schools, holiday camps and entertainments.

Such prescriptions are the norm in a materialistic society which focuses on all things physical and places more emphasis on possessions and appearances than on psychological, emotional and spiritual factors. Accordingly, a child's actual needs may be sacrificed to its parents' wants, if only because by working all hours to earn money to provide for these 'needs', the parents may rarely see the child, much less spend time with it.

MEETING OTHER PEOPLE'S NEEDS

Other people's wants are imposed upon us throughout life and often prevent us recognising, expressing and satisfying our own needs. We are all told, more or less subtly, what is wanted of us; what we should and shouldn't do. Even before we can understand language, the family begins to transmit society's messages, because its major function is to instil in us the prescribed, permitted and proscribed values of the society we live in, and acceptable and unacceptable forms of behaviour. These messages are the 'givens' of our existence, provided by others, irrespective of whether they meet our actual needs. In this way we are conditioned into believing that we need what others want us to, and as a result we tend to confuse our needs with their wants.

These messages serve as 'lifescripts' which guide our performance throughout life. Once learned they remain unquestioned and largely unchanged. They spring to mind when certain situations arise and serve as guiding rules of conduct. Instilled in the past and added to continually throughout life, these directives usually have little or no relevance to the present yet remain firmly rooted in us, unexamined, dictating the way we talk, act and express our feelings. It is therefore not surprising that most of us find it difficult to distinguish our needs from the needs and wants of others, or to perceive how much of our time and energy are taken up with attending to the latter. If we are unable to identify our needs, then we are unable to satisfy them, so unless we learn what our minds really are, a good deal of illness and suffering is inevitable.

THE LESSONS OF CHILDHOOD

Our attitudes to ourselves and the world around us are to a great extent determined by the messages our parents communicate to us in our early life. What we learn during feeding, toilet and moral training has a lasting impact on our character and behaviour because these situations present us with our first experience of conflict between fulfilling our needs and meeting the requirements of others. When parents don't respond to a child's expression of its needs, ignoring or rejecting its emotions, the child typically stops expressing itself. This inexpressive emotional style is learned very early on, usually during infancy, and this psychological pattern continues throughout life.

The disciplinary practices parents adopt are of particular importance, not only in the rewards and punishments they use but the manner in which they are given. Tangible rewards, deprivation of privileges, physical punishment and withdrawal of love are all effective in getting us to do as our parents want, but they not only produce socially conformist behaviour, they can also shape our development in such a way that our behaviour does not reflect who we truly are.

LEARNING YOUR WORTH

Children whose parents are punitive may come to believe that being loved or lovable is conditional upon exhibiting certain kinds of behaviour and feelings, and may repress, deny and distort those kinds of behaviour and feelings not positively regarded by others. If parents tell children verbally or in other ways that they and their behaviour are bad, they tend to develop negative feelings about themselves. Children whose true self is not prized, valued or approved of may come to believe that they are not loved by their parents because they are unlovable, and will begin to act in ways designed to gain approval from others. In so doing they compromise their true self, which becomes hidden, and an inauthentic or unreal self develops. This produces a division in their being, and conflict, which in turn generates tension and feelings of dis-ease and anxiety that can be manifested physically or psychologically as stress and stress-related disorders.

Those children whose parents show acceptance of them even when disapproving of particular kinds of behaviour — who say, in effect, 'I love you, even though I don't like the way you are behaving' — are more likely to develop a positive view of themselves, because if we feel our parents' appraisal of us is positive, we tend to feel good about ourselves. Our view of our own worth is therefore determined largely by how we have been treated by others. We tend to value ourselves as we are valued by them. Our authentic or true self survives when it is prized or valued by others. Free from negative evaluation, we are able to explore and express ourselves to the full, so when we are esteemed we develop a sense of self-worth which promotes the expression of our true selves. If as children we are loved and valued by our parents, we feel no need to compromise ourselves. We feel at ease with ourselves because there is little or no tension between our true self and a false one.

Ideally our parents provide us with unconditional love but in practice the love we each receive is, to varying degrees, conditional upon our ability and willingness to conform to their ambitions, hopes, expectations, desires and demands. This tends also to be true regarding all the significant people in our lives, so we learn that to be approved of and loved we have to behave ourselves by surrendering those features of ourselves which, if expressed, might cause us to lose the approval and love of others. Many of us come to believe that we cannot be ourselves and also be loved. As we cannot change our essential nature, we mask it by developing a personality which satisfies those we depend on for love. The extent to which we value the approval of others more than our true self is therefore a feature of our personality.

Our view of our own worth, or self-esteem, is not a momentary attitude or specific to certain situations but tends to be an enduring trait or personality characteristic. The sense of whether or not we are worth caring for and attending to is likely to persist throughout life. If you judge yourself unworthy, you will be less likely to care for or attend to yourself, less likely to consider your own needs or to fulfil them and more likely to be ill or unhappy as a result. You are also less likely than someone with high self-esteem to be capable of resisting pressure to conform; of achieving independence; of performing well in situations when you know you are being observed. On the other hand, you are likely to work harder for someone you perceive to be undemanding and uncritical; to feel threatened when interacting with people in positions of authority or whom you regard as in some way superior; to be influenced by persuasive communication such as strong arguments, fear-arousing appeals and prestigious endorsements; and to lack a sense of being in control. You are less likely to influence others and more likely to be concerned about personal adequacy; to think negatively about yourself; to be generally less confident and happy than you could be. You are also likely to exhibit higher levels of anxiety and tension; psychosomatic symptoms brought on by stress such as insomnia, migraine, peptic ulcers, skin complaints, hypertension, general sexual dysfunction, the whole range of neurotic disorders and depression; and to experience low energy more frequently. In short, you are more likely than someone with high self-esteem to be concerned with doing what other people want you to do than with what *you* want to do; more likely to meet their wants than to satisfy your own needs; and unlikely to express yourself authentically.

LIVING WITH TENSION

As we have seen, the way we prevent self-expression is physically — through muscle tension. Try for a moment to identify the muscles involved in stopping yourself crying. Now try to identify the muscles involved in stopping yourself from hitting out at someone. Perhaps you can see how little boys develop a stiff upper lip in trying to live up to the idea that 'big boys don't cry'; and how girls learn to keep their anger and aggression 'close to their chest'. In much the same way, the 'no' we want to utter is silenced by a clenched jaw; the punch we'd sorely like to deliver held back in our clenched fist; the cry or scream we feel like venting trapped behind tight lips; the concern we'd like to show masked by a fixed expression; the jig we'd love to dance denied by a stiff posture; the caress we long to give frozen in our rigid arms. Most of us have learned to live, to varying degrees, in a physical strait jacket that prevents us expressing ourselves lest we offend others and convention. The tension involved imposes considerable stress on the body.

STRESS

Tension is stress. The term *stress* comes from *stres* or *straisse*, Old French and Middle English words for 'adversity' or 'hardship', but, as we have seen, it is thought to originate in the Latin *stringere*, 'to draw tight'. Tension involves tightening muscles, stretching and stressing them along with ligaments and joints, which can be strained and pulled by tension that is too high. Tension also creates psychological stress because it uses up the basic chemicals present in nerve and muscle cells. Literally, therefore, sustained tension 'gets on your nerves' and can make you a 'nervous wreck' as well as wearing you out physically.

ANXIETY

Tension may be experienced psychologically as uneasiness or anxiety, which is often accompanied by a feeling of constriction, especially in the throat and chest. The sensation of tightening in these areas may lead to panic, and produce even greater tension. People with chronic tension often become locked into self-perpetuating cycles of anxiety or worry and further tension. Although tired, their muscular tension prevents them relaxing or sleeping, further exhausting them, so that action requires more and more effort and energy. As a result, they feel 'uptight', 'strung up', drained and exhausted. Such an outcome is most likely when we don't 'hold the strings' to our lives, allowing others to 'pull our strings' and control us rather than taking responsibility for ourselves.

THE CONSEQUENCES OF STRESS

Constantly trying to gain the approval of others can be very costly in terms of the stress it imposes on us both physically and psychologically, and it may not actually be effective.

Roy has tried all his life to gain the approval of others. He tries to be inconspicuous and not give offence to anyone. He is highly conventional in his dress and behaviour, speaks very quietly and moves silently on his toes. His manner is ingratiating and he never disagrees with others, yet his acquaintances do not find him agreeable. On the contrary — Roy is unpopular because in trying to please everyone at all times he is seen as two-faced and hypocritical; he is neither trusted nor respected. Roy senses other people's disapproval and tries ever harder to be liked. He is always tense and suffers from various stress-related symptoms of sufficient severity to justify his early retirement on the grounds of ill-health.

Shaping your behaviour to the requirements of others can be even more costly. Studies at Johns Hopkins University have found that bland, emotionally inexpressive people — those who say they are fine when they are not — are sixteen times more likely to develop cancers than those who feel their emotions intensely and express them.[4] Indeed the stoic, self-denying personality is the most commonly cited factor in the development of cancer. The vast literature on the psychological features of cancer patients characterises their personality in terms of related traits: denial, repression, strong commitment to social norms, and a sense of alienation stemming from early childhood experiences.

There is also evidence that perceptions of your ability to control events are critical to maintaining good mental health.[5] Those who lack a sense of personal control generally respond less favourably to stress. Indeed stressful events pose a direct challenge to both self-esteem and personal control. Feelings of effectiveness and mastery are therefore important factors in successful adjustment to stressful situations, influencing the extent to which you adopt positive forms of behaviour, with attendant benefits to your general well-being.

EXPRESSING YOURSELF

The highly influential psychiatrist Fritz Perls pointed out that for most people conformity to the demands of others is second nature. The difficulty for them is to become aware of, in touch with and responsive to their *first nature* — their authentic or true self. He argued that the *shoulds* and *should nots* of convention interfere with the healthy functioning of the organism and that it is only by being self-controlled rather than controlled by others that the authentic self or first nature can be realised.[6] Contrary to popular belief, this means expressing rather than repressing the self, by following your own intuitions, feelings and interests.

Certainly those people who express themselves fully usually rate their energy level as consistently high. Such people are usually a small minority of any group and they invariably report that they have experienced the unpleasant consequences of having not expressed themselves at one time. Joanne is typical of such people:

'I spent most of my life running around trying to be all things to all people at home and at work. I felt that I had to; that there was no alternative. I tried to convince myself I was happy but I wasn't really, and when I became seriously ill I knew I had to give up pretending to everyone else and to myself. I stopped doing everything for everyone and decided to do something for myself for a change. I realised I didn't like my job. I almost persuaded myself that I had to keep this job for the salary until I realised it was supporting a lifestyle I didn't really need or want. Everyone told me I was making a big mistake but I left the job and immediately felt better. I decided to "do my own thing" and started my own business. I enjoyed it enormously and it soon took off. Now I'm busier than ever but I'm doing something I really enjoy. I feel and look at least ten years younger. I'm in control of my life rather than being controlled by others.'

TAKING CONTROL

Each of us gives away authority over ourselves to others, to the extent that we rely on their confirmation, endorsement or validation of our thoughts, feelings, actions, beliefs and opinions rather than pleasing ourselves. Whenever we do this, we give others authority and control over us and risk losing control of ourselves and our lives.

Danny is one of five brothers. He has few childhood memories, but clearly recalls his mother stating that she and his father wanted photographs on their piano of all five sons wearing higher-degree graduands' gowns. Danny was also expected to follow in his father's professional footsteps. His own preferences, his sporting and artistic talents were all ignored or discouraged. Danny disappointed his parents by not gaining the academic standards they had set for him, and not pursuing his father's career. He often described himself as the black sheep of his family, and felt a sense of failure and inadequacy as a result. Nevertheless he achieved success in a profession he enjoyed, a happy marriage and a high standard of material comfort in life.

However, the first time that he found himself unable to perform adequately sexually, he was overwhelmed by feelings of failure, inadequacy and despair. Danny believed that he had failed his wife. He became impotent, and over a period of ten years this threatened his marriage, his mental health and eventually, as his thoughts became increasingly suicidal, his life. During this time Danny's thoughts became more and more negative. He perceived himself as worthless and a total failure. He became highly tense and anxious that he would fail in anything he attempted. He began to show signs of stress:

insomnia, palpitations and sweaty hands, and he developed persistent low back pain. He regarded himself as a victim of fate and kept asking himself, 'Why me?' It was only when in desperation he sought help with his problem that he recognised that it originated in the negative thoughts and messages he constantly relayed to himself, and was not beyond his control.

Moira describes her childhood as joyless. She cannot remember being cuddled or receiving any sign of affection from her parents. She remembers vividly the harsh treatment and constant criticism she was subjected to by her mother, and the indifference of her father. At school she realised that her tenement home was regarded by others as a slum and that she was not expected to achieve much in life. Moira became ashamed of her slovenly home and parents. She became obsessed with appearances and spent most of her time at home cleaning. When she left school she considered herself highly fortunate to be taken on as a sales assistant in a leading chain store. She worked hard, not only at her job, but also on presenting herself in an acceptable way. She changed her accent, dressed smartly, cultivated an air of refinement and professionalism, and she 'got on' — progressively working towards a top job in the company's management structure.

Moira 'got on' less well with her peers and colleagues. For some years she continued to live at home and feared making friends who would expect to be invited there. She had no boyfriends for the same reason. She later left home and moved area, but remained with the same company, which she regarded as her family, for thirty-five years. By this time she embodied the image and values of her adopted 'parent' company, appearing firmly middle-aged and middle-class, utterly respectable and absolutely middle-of-the-road. Yet there was nothing ordinary about Moira: she had no friends and although she desperately wanted to be married and have children, she had had only three relationships with men in her life. These had all foundered because she was unable to allow anyone to come close to her in case they discovered her terrible secret — her true identity. Moira remained constantly anxious that her past would be revealed and could not relax with anyone, or they with her. Tension showed in her face, posture and manner. She not only seemed totally controlled, but also as having to control everything and everyone around her.

At the age of fifty, Moira agreed to take early retirement. Without the security and meaning given to her by her job, she became severely depressed. Whereas previously she would bolster her low self-esteem by telling herself what she had achieved in life — an excellent job, the respect of her subordinates, a smart house, an expensive car and frequent holidays abroad — she could now only remind herself what she had sacrificed in doing so: friends, romance, love, marriage, children, her own life. She was full of self-loathing and fear that she would spend what remained of her life alone, but also recognised that she was totally alienated from herself. She didn't know who she really was, and no longer knew what was expected of her. She was confused and disoriented, suffered from frequent panic attacks, bouts of uncontrollable crying, chest pains, headache and various other distressing symptoms. Within a few weeks of her retirement she suffered a complete mental and physical breakdown.

Sheamus was the youngest, by several years, of three brothers and when his parents died within a year of each other the fourteen-year-old boy was told that he should 'be a man' and not show his grief. The only concession made to his loss was that he was allowed to wear a black tie. He was sent away to school soon afterwards and there this shy and sensitive boy found that he could hide his feelings behind humour and a considerable talent for mimicry. He also gained friends in this way. By the time he left school Sheamus was much in demand; he could always be relied upon to be the life and soul of the party. His performances were impressive, because far from being the highly sociable extrovert his acquaintances 'knew', he was a lonely and very sad person: a true clown. He believed that others would not like him if they really knew him. Indeed if ever he tried to be serious or to express his true feelings, he was usually told that 'this wasn't like him' and to 'get his act together'. And he did. He began to rely on alcohol to help him to perform to other people's expectations. He was encouraged to do so, because after a few drinks he became even more funny. Then he became less so. Sheamus found that when maudlin drunk — and only then — could he really express how he felt, but whatever he said was dismissed by others as the product of too much to drink.

By the age of twenty-one, Sheamus was a chronic alcoholic. Over the next twenty years he developed serious liver and brain damage, as well as kidney dysfunction, and he limped badly following several road traffic accidents when, as a driver, he had hit various obstacles or, more latterly, been hit by cars when staggering about in the road in a drunken state. He died aged forty-two from a massive brain haemorrhage, and was much mourned by his many 'friends'.

Danny and Moira both lost control of themselves and their lives, but with help managed to regain their self-control. Sheamus lost control and his life, a life not in his own hands but controlled by others.

Psychologist Larry LeShan once observed during a seminar that 'when you're holding destiny in your own hands, you're less likely to drop it'. If you are to gain *self*-control rather than be controlled by others, you have to take hold of the strings of your life. You have to learn to pull these strings yourself rather than allow them to be pulled by others. In order to do this you have let go of what you are holding on to — pent-up feelings and thoughts. You have to express yourself and allow your energy to flow. This means that you have to be able to relax the tensions that prevent this occurring. In the following chapter we will look at ways in which you can begin to identify your tensions, understand how you produce them and how you can learn to stop doing so.

KEY POINTS

1. When you express yourself, your energy flows; when you prevent self-expression, your energy is blocked by muscle tension, so your emotional blocks are also physical ones.

2. What you don't express is trapped as pent-up energy in your muscles, with the result that this energy is not available to you so you feel drained. Your energy level is an indication of the extent to which you express yourself.

3. You lose energy by meeting the demands of others rather than attending to your own needs.

4. Your needs are essential to your health and well-being and if these are neglected you will become ill, either physically or mentally.

5. The extent to which you fulfil your own needs is determined by the degree of self-worth or self-esteem you developed in childhood.

6. Your self-esteem determines to a large degree the extent to which you experience stress and your susceptibility to stress-related illness.

7. Learning to relieve stress is about developing self-awareness, recognising and acting on your own needs and being self-controlled rather than being controlled by the requirements of others. It's about getting a grip on yourself and your life.

8. You risk giving control of yourself and your life away to others every time you seek their approval, confirmation or endorsement rather than pleasing yourself.

2

LEARNING
HOW TO UNWIND

Touch one strand and the whole web trembles.
Bhagavad Gita

RELEASING TENSION

How do you relax? Watching television, reading, walking, chatting or having a few drinks with friends, cooking, gardening, listening to or playing music, knitting, participating in sporting and leisure activities are among the responses most people give to this question. So when Anne added 'flopping' to the list generated by the group she was in, she received several puzzled looks and was asked, 'How do you do that?' 'By doing nothing,' she replied, and, by way of illustration, slumped like a rag doll in her seat.

Flopping means to 'fall loosely' or 'hang loose', which is a phrase used by some people to describe the state of being relaxed. Relaxation means loosening, and as such it is the opposite of tension or tightening. It is because it involves a loosening or letting go of habitual tension that relaxation is recommended by doctors and healthcare practitioners as an antidote to chronic tension and the resulting low energy and fatigue. Whereas tension involves *doing* something, relaxation is *non-doing* — not doing anything. This is difficult for most of us to achieve because we are conditioned to think we should be doing something all the time and are wasting time if we are not. The prescription 'just relax' is one of the most difficult to put into practice, although relaxation is, by definition, ease itself. Most of us are doing something at all times, even when we don't think that we are. We don't realise that we are habitually tense or the extent of this tension. We may believe we are relaxed or relaxing when in fact we are not.

Relaxation is not achieved simply by lying in bed, lounging in front of the television or being idle. It is an integrated shift in physiological functioning that is rarely, if ever, achieved without training and practice. You may think that you're relaxed when lying quietly on a sofa, and may appear to be so, but even after several hours no significant physiological changes may have occurred. Even when you feel relaxed, deep-seated muscular tension may remain and be revealed in the form of irregular breathing, elevated pulse rate, involuntary or localised reflex actions such as wrinkling of the forehead, tight facial muscles, blinking and swallowing. When you are truly relaxed all tension is absent, breathing is regular, the pulse rate is low, limbs lack firmness, are soft, limp and floppy. You do not constantly blink or swallow.

ACQUIRING MUSCLE SENSE

In order to relax you need to know not only that you are tense but also where exactly the tension is located, and how you are producing and maintaining it. Only then can you stop being tense and begin to relax. The first step towards relaxation is therefore achieving simple bodily awareness, or muscle sense.

Bodily awareness focuses attention on something we all do easily and habitually — tightening our muscles — on the principle that when you realise what tension is and how you tense or tighten a muscle, you can just as easily relax or loosen it. Many relaxation procedures therefore involve learning to identify tension in muscles of the body by first tightening them and then ceasing to do so. In this way we can train the body to react in the desired manner when required. You may like to try the following simple exercise.

EXERCISE ONE

LOOSENING UP AND LETTING GO OF YOUR TENSION

Find somewhere you can sit or lie comfortably. Close your eyes or focus on a fixed point such as a mark on the wall or floor. Gradually bring your attention from your surroundings to the boundary between your body and the surfaces adjacent to it. As you do so, notice whether the contact is comfortable or painful, and adjust your position so as to maximise comfort and minimise pain.

When you are positioned as comfortably as possible, focus your attention on your toes. Tighten them for a few seconds and then let go of the tightness, noticing its effect not simply on your toes and feet but also on the rest of your body. Repeat this once or twice and then move your attention to your lower legs and do likewise, tightening the muscles there, holding that tightness for a few seconds before letting go of it and observing the effect on the rest of your body.

Then work your way upwards, tightening and loosening each of the major areas of your body in turn: your thighs, buttocks, lower back, stomach, chest, shoulders, arms, hands, neck, face and jaw. If any parts of your body remain tense, tight or painful, spend a few minutes alternately tightening and loosening them until you feel an overall reduction of tightness in your body.

Having done this, once again focus attention on your toes. Tighten them, and while still doing so proceed to tighten your thighs, buttocks, lower back, stomach, chest, shoulders, arms, hands, neck, face and jaw so that your muscles become progressively tighter from the tip of your toes to the point of your jaw. Continue to tighten your muscles until your entire body has become quite rigid. Hold this stiffness for a few moments and then let go of it. Take a few moments to experience the sensation throughout your body. If you have been really tightening your muscles, your body should feel quite floppy once you let go.

REACTIONS TO THE EXERCISE

Interpersonal Tension

You will probably find that this procedure helps you to identify areas of muscle tension and pain. You may have felt fairly comfortable and thought you were relaxed until you focused attention on specific muscles and realised just how tense many of them were. Claire speaks for many people when she says, 'Despite thinking I was relaxed, I was in fact still very tense.' When Linda tried this exercise in a group, her throat dried and she began to cough. The more she tried to stop, the more she coughed until she felt she had to leave the room so that others wouldn't be disturbed. She had no difficulty when she tried the exercise alone later and realised that she is always tense and self-conscious when in the company of others, even friends.

Being 'Uptight'

You may have been surprised by the degree of tension you identified. This is by no means uncommon. Darren, for example, only realised how tense he was when he found that he couldn't make many of his muscles tighter than they already were. You too may have identified specific areas of tension you weren't previously aware of. Richard discovered that his neck and shoulders were already very tight, and realised that he suffers from aches and pains in these parts when he feels under pressure. Like many people, he is literally 'uptight'.

Identifying areas of tension in this way may in itself enable you to reduce tension there. Julie found that her tension was mainly located in her head, and with daily practice she was able to relax these muscles and eliminate the severe tension headaches she had suffered for many years. Sometimes the existing tension in a muscle group is such that any attempt to tighten that area produces pain. It may also produce insights — as Brenda discovered:

'When I performed the exercise, I felt a sharp pain as I tightened the calf of my right leg. When I turned my head from side to side, it felt very heavy and stiff and I thought it was going to be impossible to move. I experienced a short, shooting pain between my shoulder blades and this seemed to lighten the weight of my head to a small extent and I was able to turn my head each way, but this still required effort. I feel this strain is a representation of the fact that I often "carry a burden" on my shoulders and have the "troubles of the world" there. I am an eldest child and as I grew up I was left with responsibility for my siblings and often the blame for their actions, and now as an adult I feel a burden of responsibilities towards my parents. The sharp pain could be an indication that, although it might feel painful to let go of my responsibilities to some degree, it would give me some freedom.'

Painful Tensions

Stephen also made a startling discovery during this exercise. As he experienced a releasing of tension throughout his body, he became aware of pain in his stomach: 'It seemed my mind and body were at this point fixed on this area of pain.' Initially he tried to dismiss this, but each time he attempted the exercise he experienced the same pain. He then realised that his habitually high level of tension masked this pain, which on medical investigation proved to be a gastric ulcer.

Pain or infirmity may prevent one from being able to make

the muscular contractions required in this kind of exercise. Patricia, who suffered the painful after-effects of a whiplash injury to her neck, found the very prospect of tensing it created anxiety and prevented her attempting to do so. Karen, who was quite unsettled during the exercise, shifting about trying to find a comfortable position, realised that she was trying to avoid the constant pressure and pain of a long-standing neck injury which she had become so accustomed to she was beginning not to notice. As with Stephen, muscular tension in that area was masking the problem. Once she was aware of it, Karen sought treatment for the condition, which proved effective. Tensions that we create in order to protect painful injuries are often maintained long after the initial injury has healed, producing long-standing and sometimes chronic pain and disability disproportionate to the original problem.

Boredom

Some people find that this kind of relaxation procedure that focuses on muscle tensing is tedious, and painfully boring rather than physically painful. You too may have found yourself becoming impatient or bored, and more tense as a result — literally 'bored stiff'. If this was the case, then Exercise Two, below, may be easier for you. Nevertheless it might be a good idea to pause and ask yourself what you were so impatient to do that prevented you relaxing.

Kelly wanted to race through the exercise. She didn't have the patience to do it properly but realised that this indicated her inability to slow down:

> 'I feel that I cannot relax or de-stress at the moment as there is always something that needs to be done and never enough time to do everything I should do. Through this exercise I realised I have to find time to relax.'

People like Kelly are always hoping that they will 'find' time rather than have to make or take time for relaxation. If you can identify with Kelly, it may be a worthwhile asking yourself whose *shoulds* these are, whether you actually *need* to do anything about them, and why you feel that you *must*.

Tension, Anxiety and Panic

A further drawback of relaxation procedures that focus on muscle tightening is that they can create greater tension and anxiety. Most people find it much easier to tighten their muscles than to loosen them, so that when they increase the tension in their body they then tend to retain it. This is particularly true of those people who most need to learn how to relax. Their overall level of tension is therefore increased rather than reduced and may be accompanied by anxiety, panic or other unpleasant feelings.

Mike, for instance, experienced a dramatic spiralling of tension when the existing tension in his stomach region was exaggerated, producing feelings of nausea. These in turn generated anxiety that he might vomit, and further anxiety as he tried to bring the anxiety and unpleasant physical sensations under control.

As a result of the increased tension involved, you too may be unable to relax using procedures that focus primarily on muscle tension. Even if you can achieve relaxation in this way, you may experience sudden anxiety or even panic. This is because the sensations associated with relaxation — wooziness, lightness, falling, floating, vibrations, tingling and loss of sensation in the limbs — appear strange if you have rarely or never experienced them before.

Deep Breathing

Deep breathing is often recommended as a way of reducing tension, pain and anxiety. As we have seen, tension tightens and narrows the chest and throat, resulting in shallow breathing. In principle, attempting to breathe deeply should reverse the process as it requires a relaxation of tension in these areas. In practice, however, it often does quite the opposite. Uncertainty about where to focus when attending to breathing can generate anxiety and increased tension. When Jane concentrated on her breathing, she found that her chest tightened and this induced a sense of panic. Her experience is not unusual. More typically, however, people find that their attention is diverted from their breathing by intrusive thoughts and they may become anxious because of their inability to focus.

Worrying about being unable to relax often makes people more tense. Many people are like Tom:

> 'I started to worry, not desperately, just a nagging suspicion that I might be a raving neurotic so centred on myself I might be incapable of letting go. I decided not to panic — yet. Once I realised that it isn't unusual to get these feelings of frustration, to not be able to do it instantly, I could relax.'

Even if you have not experienced any of these difficulties, you will probably find that Exercise Two enables you to relax more easily and fully. Try it, and compare the process and outcome with those of Exercise One.

EXERCISE TWO

RELAXING BY BREATHING LIGHTLY

Find somewhere to sit comfortably. Become aware of how your body is located in relation to its surroundings. Then close your eyes or focus on a fixed point or object within your line of vision, such as a mark on the wall, ceiling or floor. Now, gradually draw your attention from your surroundings and bring it to the boundary between your body and the surfaces adjacent to it. As you do so, notice whether the contact is uncomfortable or painful, and adjust your position so as to maximise comfort and minimise pain.

When you are positioned as comfortably as possible, focus attention on the tip of your nose. Imagine that you are breathing coloured light in through your nose. This enters your body and is drawn into and through your head then down to the base of your spine where it curls upwards. As you breathe out it is drawn upwards, forcing a dark dense fog towards and out of your mouth, leaving your body feeling light and clear. Continue breathing in this way for a few minutes.

REACTIONS TO THE EXERCISE
Imagining Breath as Light

By itself breathing through the nose slows and deepens your breathing and produces greater relaxation. Nevertheless it has a major drawback in that, initially at least, it may not be sufficiently absorbing to hold your attention. Imagining that you are breathing in light or colour is much more absorbing for most people and promotes relaxation more easily.

Pam suffers from asthma. Breathing exercises normally make her tense because she fears she will have an asthma attack, yet she found that imagining golden light was so absorbing and soothing that it overcame her worries and she was able to relax without difficulty.

This exercise also often provides valuable insights, as Claire's experience shows:

'When imagining breathing light in through my nose, I couldn't see the light passing through my head. Instead it went straight down the back of my throat and round the bottom of my skull. While I felt relaxed, the light simply refused to go through my head. Afterwards I was asked if I suffer from tension headaches. I do suffer from headaches but had never associated them with tension. I could then relate the tension in my skull, especially at the base, to the headaches, and now when I feel tension beginning to mount, I relax myself and allow the energy to flow through my head. I have not had any headaches since using this method and I have found it a far more effective way of dealing with my problem than using drugs.'

Jane makes a similar observation:

'I felt energy blocked at the top of my head and shoulders. This is significant because I think that is where work stress manifests itself, because I'm always thinking about it and carrying a big workbag on my shoulders.'

These accounts show that this exercise is good for identifying areas where energy is blocked by tension.[1] However, it doesn't necessarily provide insight into why energy is being blocked there. You will probably find that the following exercise increases your awareness of those aspects of yourself that your tensions prevent you from expressing.

EXERCISE THREE

RELAXING WITH IMAGERY

Find somewhere to sit comfortably and, having done so, become aware of how your body is located in relation to its surroundings. Then close your eyes or focus on a fixed point or object within your line of vision, such as a mark on the wall, ceiling or floor. Having done so, gradually withdraw your attention from your surroundings and bring it to the boundary between your body and the surfaces adjacent to it. As you do this, notice whether the contact is uncomfortable or painful, and adjust your position so as to maximise comfort and minimise pain.

When you are positioned as comfortably as possible, bring

your attention to your right arm, then down your arm into your right hand. Imagine that you are holding in that hand an ancient gold coin. It is the only one of its kind known to exist and is therefore priceless. Grip your imaginary coin so tightly that there is no possibility of it slipping from your hand, and as you do so observe the effects of this action, not only in your hand, lower arm, upper arm and shoulder but also in your neck, head, jaw, chest and elsewhere in your body. Follow the effects of this tightening as far as they extend and until you can feel a tremor developing in your arm. When this occurs, or if the action is becoming too painful or unpleasant to sustain, carefully transfer the coin to your left hand, once again gripping it so tightly that there is no danger of it being lost. Follow the effect to its furthest extremity and tighten your grip until you can feel a tremor in your arm. When you can feel this, toss the coin from the left hand to the right and then throw it away, allowing the fingers of both hands to drop loosely as you do so, and your arms to fall by your sides.

Now imagine that the floor beneath you is beginning to rise. Resist this as forcefully as you can, spreading the fingers and palms of your hands flat and pushing downwards. The floor continues to rise, forcing your hands upwards and obliging you to flex you arms against it. Despite this, the floor continues to rise, until, just as it seems you can resist no further, the floor falls away and your arms and hands with it. Allow your arms to flop at your side. Take a minute or so to experience this sensation of floppiness and allow it to spread throughout your body.

When you have done so, bring your attention to your stomach. Imagine that you have a large red plastic clown's nose held there by a piece of elastic, and that as you breathe in and out you can see it moving backwards and forwards. Breathe in and out deeply for a few minutes, watching the red nose and noting your reactions.

Now imagine that, like a puppet, you have strings attached to your shoulders, arms and hands, and to the top of your head, and that slowly and steadily these strings are being pulled so that your head, shoulders, upper body, arms and hands are being drawn steadily upwards. Your spine is extending along its full length, your lower back arching and your thighs and legs flexing as you are pulled upwards. At the same time your chin is rising upwards and away from your neck, tilting backwards and then slightly forward as your head rises.

Just as you begin to rise out of your seat, the strings are cut and your body flops down on the chair like a rag doll, your arms hanging loosely by your sides. Focus for a few moments on these feelings of floppiness and allow them to spread throughout your body. Also note any new insight or awareness that may have occurred during the exercise.

REACTIONS TO THE EXERCISE

Relaxing Imagery

Even though this exercise focuses on muscle tightening, you will probably find it easier and that you feel more relaxed by it than Exercise One. Most people relax much more easily and quickly when relaxation procedures engage their imaginative faculties. This is because when focusing on images they tend to forget about trying to relax and as a result they relax effortlessly. The images provide a focus for both mental and muscular activity and enable you to become more absorbed. This makes the experience more complete and often produces significant reactions. (The therapeutic use of visual imagery is covered in more detail in the next chapter.)

Emotional Release

You may have experienced a sudden release of emotion when you imagined letting go of the coin. Crying, feeling overwhelmingly sad or angry are all common reactions to this image. This is because tension holds in feelings so that they won't be expressed. When this tension is relaxed, the feelings held in — whether emotions or physical sensations — are often also released; as are memories and other mental images. The feelings and memories are often painful because, when we experience pain or hurt, we defend ourselves against future trauma of this kind by contracting various muscles.

The psychotherapist Wilhelm Reich termed this defensive behaviour pattern *muscle armouring*. He observed that if we maintain these tensions over time, they come to characterise us, becoming structural components of our character. These *character structures*, as Reich referred to them, are reflected in our posture and in our entire behaviour, and often set up patterns of dysfunction and disease. When we begin to relax these muscles, the feelings they are defending are released spontaneously, so as we loosen up physically we may also experience a release of held-in or pent-up emotions. This release of tension achieves what psychotherapists refer to as *catharsis* or *abreaction*: a sudden awareness of repressed emotions, experiences or ideas. In addition to emotions, we may also experience thoughts, impressions or images related to the circumstances that initially provoked the defensive response; a person, place, situation or object might spontaneously spring to mind.[2]

Holding on to the imaginary coin often produces responses that provide an insight not only into the emotions we holding in, but also what we are holding on to, or trying to maintain a grip on in life.

Letting go of the coin is often accompanied by an upswelling of memories of loss and feelings of sadness, as well as sudden insights. Jane describes her experience as follows:

> 'Immediately I let go of the coin, I had a strong image of my grandmother who died recently. It was so strong and unexpected I began to cry. The exercise showed me that I haven't yet properly come to terms with her death and that it will take time to do so.'

Gill experienced a similar insight:

> 'It was my family I was afraid to loose [*sic*]. My father is old and ill and my daughters are about to leave the nest. Although I have rationalised these "losses" and may be prepared for these events mentally, evidently I am not yet prepared emotionally.' [Note that Gill wrote 'loose' rather than 'lose' here.]

Sometimes there are no accompanying images, only inexplicable feelings. Brenda was puzzled to find that although the coin felt very safe in her right hand, she was very unsure and hesitant about transferring it to her left hand. Once transferred it felt extremely unsafe and she experienced a great sense of relief when she threw it away. Thinking about these feelings later, she realised that her financial situation dictates the choices in her life. She feels very uncomfortable about this, as she knows she is not a material person and despises the burdens money often creates, so would like to rid herself of this restriction.

Carole's experience shows that powerful insights can occur as a result of the images that arise in association with the act of letting go:

> 'In this exercise I learned an extremely valuable lesson and, I feel, was provided with a sense of enlightenment about my own emotions. I held in my right hand the most precious coin in the world. I gripped it as tightly as I possibly could, tensing my whole arm, neck and shoulder to achieve maximum effect. When I transferred my coin to the left hand, I was surprised to find that my right side was as tense as when I was holding the coin in my right hand. I had a vision of dangling over the edge of a cliff and I knew that if I let my right side relax, I would plunge into the rock-strewn ocean below. I was aware of someone standing over me — a man — and he was laughing at my

fear. The fear I felt wasn't of the man but of falling to certain death.

'The only time I have ever felt this way was when I was sexually attacked by someone I believed to be a work colleague and friend. It occurred to me that, despite having consciously resolved the issue, I had not resolved how it made me feel or how it had impacted on other aspects of my life. This was the first time I realised that when attacked I had actually been in fear of my life. As I was an army officer and fear is not an emotion you are supposed to feel, I had never acknowledged the fear to myself, let alone anyone else. During the resulting prosecution I felt my sense of justice was sacrificed to save a senior member of staff. Only when I could admit these things to myself could I finally let go of the coin.'

Difficulty in Letting Go

Letting go of the coin is often quite difficult for some people, especially if you habitually defend yourself against loss, albeit unconsciously. Angela's experience illustrates this difficulty well:

'When gripping the coin, I felt pain. I also felt this was very significant as the coin represented the most valuable thing in the world. I feel that my attitude to holding the coin reflects my defensive and sometimes self-destructive approach to various aspects of my life. I feel that it may represent the fear I have of holding on to important things too tightly in case I lose them. Rather than have this happen, I find it preferable to discard them myself and so prevent myself being hurt as a result of losing unexpectedly things that are important to me.'

Reluctance to let go of the coin may give rise to other feelings — as it did for Anya:

'When I had to throw the coin away, I became quite indignant. The coin was mine and I was not prepared to throw it away. I didn't want to throw it away so I decided to keep it and pretend I had thrown it away. I realised only later that the coin represented the anger and resentment I hold towards my natural father. I have had no form of contact with him since he and my mother separated when I was four. My refusal to throw the coin away represents my belief that my anger towards my father is justified. More disturbingly, however, it is indicative of the fact that I don't want to stop being angry with him. I had a choice whether or not I threw the coin away; I can also stop being angry with my father. I have found this difficult to digest because it makes me realise that I am responsible for my reaction. Being a passive victim is in one sense actually quite comfortable: it relinquishes me of responsibility. On the other hand, the knowledge that I do have some control in this situation is empowering. While I cannot change the past, I am free to alter the effect I allow it to have on my present. Having energy trapped in the past makes life difficult. By ceasing to hold on to negative emotions of the past, I can release energy into the present.'

Resistance

You are less likely to experience images associated with resisting the rising floor. The main function of this part of the exercise, apart from assisting the build-up and release of overall tension (for which it is most effective), is to highlight the effects of resistance on our bodies. Most of us are resistant to and actively resisting some features of our lives without being aware of the fact and how it characteristically manifests itself in us. A considerable amount of our energy on an everyday basis goes into either resisting the pressures imposed on us by others, or trying to overcome their resistance to us (see Chapter Seven). This is often the reason why we feel inexplicably drained or worn out when we are with our families or work colleagues. The more familiar the sensations induced by this part of the exercise, the more likely it is that you habitually carry a lot resistance around with you. The same applies if you suffer frequent aches and pains in your arms, shoulders, chest, neck and jaw. You may also gain insights from the exercise, however; as did Jan, who realised that much of her energy is drained by keeping others 'at arm's length'.

Fear of Appearing Silly

Reactions to the clown's nose are invariably interesting. Many people find this part of the exercise very amusing but few, if any of them, actually express their amusement. They resist doing so, and when asked why, usually say that they didn't want to appear stupid or silly, even when doing the exercise alone. In itself this response gives an indication of the extent to which self-expression is sacrificed on the altar of social conformity. Even though we may laugh or chuckle fairly frequently, few of us allow ourselves a real 'belly laugh' because the associated physical reactions of a heaving stomach and sides, streaming eyes, doubled-up posture and falling about are usually deemed unseemly and out of place. When we relax this control, we may release a belly laugh and so defend ourselves against this possibility by tensing that region.

However, this part of the exercise does not necessarily provoke amusement, as Paul's experience reveals:

'Up until this moment I felt relaxed. However, this particular aspect of the exercise was quite disconcerting. I was unable to settle and my breathing became shallow. I felt tense and physically uncomfortable and remained so until the image disappeared. Talking about the exercise later, I recalled a family joke which focused disdainfully on the clown-like red noses that could be attached to radiator grilles of cars. Quite ridiculously, the joke developed so that eventually I became irritated by the sight of these objects — but also felt guilty because of the charity they represented. It was interesting that this long-forgotten series of events physically manifested itself during the exercise. It highlighted for me an association between personal history and stress, and how, for me, the link could be problematic. As a person who feels occasionally stressed for no apparent reason, the focus this imagery provides has made me aware of triggers in the environment, and how these can relate to memory-events. Consequently the issues can be addressed and the stress eradicated. Once I know why I am suffering, the suffering subsides. I have learned from this exercise the strong relationship between mental and physical well-being and that self-awareness can reduce physical problems.'

Being 'All Strung Up'

Many people find that imagining themselves as a puppet whose strings have been cut enables them to 'flop' very easily. This part of the exercise is an element used in a highly effective relaxation procedure known as Autogenic Training (see Chapter Four). However, in some cases the puppet imagery prevents relaxation. Kath imagined that she fell into many pieces when the strings supporting her were cut. She subsequently realised that her fear of 'falling apart' and 'going to pieces' if she relaxed or 'let herself go' kept her tense. In effect tension throughout her entire body defended her against this possibility. Not surprisingly, therefore, she had great difficulty relaxing.

Sarah also had a problem with this part of the exercise:

'I found myself feeling quite uncomfortable with this image and realised that it was because I didn't know who was at the other end of the strings, pulling them. I didn't like the idea of another person having control over me.'

Sarah's response is interesting because it betrays some confusion. She was producing the image of the strings being pulled. She was therefore in control of them, and could have chosen not to pull them or not to cut them. She could also have shown, as part of that image, who or what was pulling them. But she seems unaware of these choices and to believe that she is a passive, albeit indignant, subject of external control. This tendency to attribute what psychologists call the *locus* of control to others — to imagine that they are 'pulling the strings' rather than oneself — correlates very highly with the experience of stress and feelings of helplessness and hopelessness. Sarah's experience provides a graphic illustration that this tendency produces uncomfortable feelings or tension and makes it difficult to relax.

Identifying Energy Blocks

As these illustrations show, all parts of the above exercise can help you to identify tensions in your body and may provide valuable insights into contributory factors. You may also discover that the exercise affords you some relief from your tensions. However, you will probably find that the following exercise is particularly effective in helping you to release the major energy blocks in your body.

EXERCISE FOUR

DISSOLVING YOUR TENSIONS AND ANXIETY

Find somewhere you can sit or lie comfortably. Having done so, close your eyes or focus on a fixed point. Imagine that you are outdoors on a warm sunny day. The heat from the sun is pleasant and you can feel its rays warming but not burning your body. As you become aware of your body and sensations within it, identify areas of tension, discomfort or pain. Imagine these in the form of ice. As you focus your attention on each of these areas in turn, imagine that the sun's rays are penetrating your body and melting the ice. Your tensions, discomforts and pains dissolve, first into a drop and then a trickle, and eventually into a stream of fluid that flows through and out of your body leaving it feeling pleasantly warm and heavy.

When your bodily tensions have disappeared, focus on your head. Imagine that the sun's rays are penetrating your mind and dissolving your mental tensions and anxieties. They too flow away through and out of your body, leaving your mind clear. Allow yourself a few minutes to observe and experience the flow within you.

Claire is typical of the many people who have found the above exercises highly effective. As she explains:

> 'I have since learned to recognise tension and take positive steps to control it before it manifests itself in other ways. I now appreciate that relaxation is far more than simply resting. I find that I am not as irritable or as frenzied as I was, because I can deal with stress as it arises rather than allowing it to control me. I feel more in control of my life, and now make the time to relax, not only in body but also in mind.'

In other words, Claire is beginning to learn how to pull her own strings rather than have them pulled for her.

KEY POINTS

1. Relaxation involves letting go tension and releasing pent-up energy. To achieve it requires training and practice, and the acquisition of muscle 'sense'.
2. Relaxation exercises help you to identify the areas of tension in your body.

3. They can also help you to identify the ways in which you characteristically defend yourself against anxiety and painful emotions.
4. They can help you to release repressed emotions.
5. Exercises incorporating visual imagery can be more effective in helping you to relax than approaches that focus solely on muscle contractions and breathing.
6. The use of visual imagery can also highlight issues and circumstances you typically respond to by becoming tense.
7. It can promote important insights and self-awareness that help you to understand the stress you experience both physically and psychologically.
8. The insights derived from relaxation exercises can help you to relieve and overcome pain and discomfort, headache and other stress-related symptoms, anxiety and low self-confidence.

3

ACKNOWLEDGING YOUR HANG-UPS

What an absurd amount of energy I have been wasting all my life trying to figure out how things 'really are' when all the time they weren't.
Hugh Prather, *Notes to Myself*

STRESS AND THE IMAGINATION

Brian was dismayed when, in the first of a series of classes on stress management, I explained the importance of relaxation. As he said:

> 'I've tried every kind of relaxation procedure, and I can get my body so relaxed that I can no longer even feel it, but as soon as I do, my Access statement and overdraft come to mind; I imagine my bank manager and immediately I tense up again.'

You would have to be Inspector Clouseau not to recognise the main source of stress in Brian's life! We may not all share his financial concerns but we all share to some degree his basic problem, which is that our head rules our body, and what is in our head determines the extent to which we experience stress. Our thoughts, concerns, conflicts, fears and anxieties generate physical tensions, and we cannot fully relax our bodies unless we are able to relax or let go of these. Focusing solely on physical relaxation, which characterises many stress-management programmes, tends to obscure the fact that bodily tensions are generated in response to mental and emotional tensions, and that if these are not eased, physical relaxation will prove difficult or, at best, limited.

It is the way we see and think about the world — our attitude to life — as well as the beliefs we have about it that determine the level of stress we experience. Brian's comment shows that our imagination can also be a source of stress. Fears, anxieties and dread are often responses to our worst imaginings rather than to actual happenings, and many of them relate not to life-threatening or dangerous situations but to everyday, ordinary events. We may fear that no one likes us, that we will not succeed at examination or interview; that we will fail to attract friends and lovers; that we will lose our job or our loved ones; develop painful or debilitating illnesses; and so on. Much of the stress we experience is undoubtedly a product of our imagination, determined by events, circumstances and things that are not externally real. Nevertheless the stress our imagination produces and the psychological and physical effects of this are very real.

THE PHYSICAL EFFECTS OF STRESS

Stress is a term used in engineering to mean any force that causes change. The specific changes caused by stress are referred to as *strain*, which, like the word *tension*, means to 'draw or stretch tight'. In engineering it is recognised that if structures or systems are subjected to excessive stress, they will break down, but that different structures will respond differently to stress, depending on their physical composition or character.

Earlier this century, the term *stress* was adopted by physiologists to refer to bodily changes that occur in humans and animals — specifically the physical reactions known as 'fight' or 'flight' responses which prepare one either to avoid or confront potentially dangerous and life-threatening situations. These are the body's 'red alert' systems which prepare it to take action to avoid potential injury and death.

Irrespective of whether you confront or flee from danger, the same bodily changes occur. These involve tension or tightening of the muscles throughout the body to prepare it for confrontation or taking evasive action. The chest and throat also tighten and narrow so that breathing becomes shallow and rapid in order to supply more oxygen to the muscles. The level of certain hormones — notably adrenaline (known in the US as epinephrine), which releases stored sugars — rises, releasing extra sugar into the blood to provide sufficient energy for speedy action.

Another hormone, norephinephrine, which increases heart rate and blood pressure, is produced causing blood to be pumped quickly to the muscles, as is cortisol which helps the body prepare for vigorous activity. Fats and cholesterol are released into the blood together with chemicals to make the blood clot more rapidly in the event of injury. In order to cool the body, perspiration increases. Meanwhile all processes not immediately essential to survival are suspended. So salivation and digestion slow down as extra blood is directed to muscles and the brain. These changes are experienced as stiffness in various parts of the body, especially the back and neck; tightness in the neck, which may feel like a lump in the throat, and in the chest; heart pounding; butterflies in the stomach; sweating; and a dry mouth. Once danger has passed, though, the body quickly returns to normal.

These reactions are essential to survival, and as such are healthy. They are unhealthy only if they are triggered repeatedly in response to non-threatening situations and so become habitual. The body then remains in a continually reactive state. Muscles stay tense; pulse rate and blood pressure remain elevated; high levels of sugars, fats, cholesterol, hormones and other chemicals persist in the blood; and the digestive processes are inactivated. Over time this state of dis-ease leads to the wear and tear of various body organs and inevitably takes its toll on health. It may result in cardiovascular problems, stroke, heart attack, kidney failure, gastro-intestinal disorders, diabetes and much else. It can, and all too frequently does, prove deadly.

STRESS-RELATED DISEASE

The link between stress and cancer has long been established. Stress has also been identified as a major factor in hypertension and all the associated complaints (see below), migraine and tension headaches, constipation, menstrual difficulties, chronic backache, ulcers and gastro-intestinal conditions, allergies, pruritis, asthma, vertigo, arthritis, hypothyroidism, multiple schlerosis, diabetes and tuberculosis. It is also recognised as a factor in skin disorders such as dermatitis, eczema and psoriasis, and is implicated in diseases related to smoking, eating disorders, alcohol and drug abuse.

In order to understand how life-threatening conditions can result from stress, we need only to examine one element of the stress reaction — raised blood pressure.

Hypertension

Sustained high blood pressure, or hypertension, is a very dangerous condition in which the blood vessels throughout the body are made smaller and smaller by constant contraction of the smooth muscles in their walls. Once it develops it will continue throughout adulthood unless treated. However, because the disease itself causes no physical discomfort, it remains undetected in many people until they develop symptoms or become ill. Fewer than one in eight people with hypertension are treated effectively. This is not simply through lack of detection. The treatment of hypertension involves drugs that produce side-effects such as dizziness, a dry mouth, impaired sexual functioning and impotence, constipation, depression, nausea, vomiting and severe diarrhoea. In many cases the side-effects of anti-hypertensive drugs are so unpleasant that patients stop taking them, which is one of the reasons why physicicans increasingly prefer to recommend stress-reduction techniques involving relaxation. However, the long-term effects of hypertension are much worse than the effects of medication.

Cardiovascular Disease

The damage caused by prolonged hypertension is substantial. Widespread cardiovascular disease is one of the long-term effects. Since the blood volume in the system remains constant, some vessels carry blood under greater pressure than they would if there were no constriction of blood vessels. As a result the pressure on the vessel walls is greatly increased and if sustained causes them to weaken and tear. When this occurs cholesterol plaques are formed to repair the damage. If there is an excessive number of these plaques, the vessels become narrower and narrower, creating further pressure and possibly leading to further tears. Pressure also increases because these plaques cause the arteries to harden and become less flexible. Plaques can also become easily detached from the arterial walls and cause further blockage in the blood supply to the heart muscles or create a dangerous situation in which clots are likely to form.

Heart Failure

Raised blood pressure also affects the heart directly as it must work harder to pump blood throughout the body under increased resistance. The left ventricle of the heart is frequently adversely affected. It becomes larger and may become abnormally distended when cardiovascular disease is advanced. Ultimately its functioning deteriorates and signs of heart failure appear.

Arteriosclerosis, Coronary Heart Disease and Cerebral Stroke

The condition in which cholesterol deposits accumulate in the arteries is known as arteriosclerosis and in the developed world it claims more lives annually than any other disease. As the cholesterol plaques decay and die, they can rupture. When this occurs the circulating blood reaching it begins to clot. If the plaque area is large, a dangerously big blood clot can form and this is the cause of most coronary heart attacks and cerebral strokes, which occur when normal circulation to the heart or brain respectively is cut off by a clot. Death in these cases is often sudden. Even if their effects are not fatal, clots may cause tissue to degenerate in the kidneys and may also give rise to ulcers and gangrene in the legs.

Heart Attack

Arteriosclerosis is also the usual cause of heart attack, or myocardial infarction, and most frequently attacks the left coronary artery. When this artery narrows, the possibility of a blood clot becoming trapped and blocking the constricted vessel increases. If such a blockage occurs, the flow of blood to the heart is arrested and prevents it functioning. The areas of the heart starved of blood die, never to recover, and depending on the size and location of the dead tissue, or infarct, the heart's owner may also die. If the infarct is detected and treated quickly, the person may survive with severe or only slight impairment of the heart's function.

Congestive Heart Failure

Blockage of the coronary arteries also causes congestive heart failure. Here the entire left ventricle of the heart becomes increasingly weak owing to blood and oxygen starvation resulting from narrowed arteries, and blood accumulates in the lungs. Excessive blood in the lungs results in shortness of breath and eventually failure of the right ventricle, which leads to swelling of the liver and the limbs.

Hypertension affects major organs other than the heart, notably the brain and the kidneys.

Brain Damage

In addition to the temporary or permanent brain damage that results from cerebral stroke which hypertension causes by way of arteriosclerosis, the brain is also affected directly through brain haemorrhage caused by high blood pressure bursting blood vessels.

Renal Disease

The kidneys usually control blood pressure, but when diseased by hypertension they raise blood pressure further. Normally if blood pressure decreases to low levels, the kidneys' adrenal glands secrete hormones that increase it. They can be thought of as sensors that monitor and maintain adequate blood pressure. However, if arteriosclerosis develops in the blood vessels of the kidneys, these shrink and become blocked. This leads to low blood pressure in the kidneys, which respond by secreting hormones and raising blood pressure in the body. A vicious cycle is established because raising the blood pressure leads to further arteriosclerosis that further blocks blood flow to the kidneys, and results in further increases in blood pressure. Some of the excess hormones that the adrenal glands release can also interfere with the functioning of the body's immune system.

Suppression of the Immune System

The immune system consists of more than a dozen different kinds of white blood cells — concentrated in the spleen, thymus gland and lymph nodes — which circulate the entire body through the blood and lymphatic system. They are divided into two types: the B-cells which produce chemicals that neutralise toxins made by disease-inducing organisms and help the body mobilise its own defences; and the T-cells and their helpers, — killer cells that destroy invading bacteria and viruses. Both are controlled by the brain, either directly through hormones in the blood stream, or indirectly through the nerves and neuro-chemicals. In emergency situations the primary action of the adrenal hormones is to suppress the work of the immune system. Immunity is placed 'on hold' while the body's energies are used to fight immediate crises. When stress reactions are prolonged, so too is this immuno-suppression. Hence what is in the short term an adaptive response can eventually become the cause of every conceivable disease involving the immune system.

However, the massive changes sustained during periods of prolonged stress go far beyond immune activity to affect every gland in the body and the processes involved in the reproduction, growth, integrity and well-being of the body at the cellular level. Unsurprisingly, 75 per cent of all illness is estimated to be stress-related.

IDENTIFYING STRESS

Many people who are dis-eased often do not realise it until clinical symptoms such as hypertension are diagnosed or they become ill. They have grown accustomed to the symptoms of stress and for them such feelings are normal. Not only are such people usually unaware that they are stressed but they often do not know what is stressing them.

Shafa, a young man in his early twenties, was shocked when his doctor told him he was suffering from hypertension and puzzled when he was asked what was stressing him. He thought he was coping well with his life and could identify no specific sources of stress. It was several months later when he was relaxing on a beach during his first holiday for some years that Shafa realised that he dreaded returning to work. Until then he had not recognised how over-pressured he was by work or identified the aspects of it that were particularly stressful. He resolved to take it easy in future and within a few months his blood pressure returned to normal.

In some instances the symptoms of stress escalate quite dramatically, producing panic. Father Bernard is an elderly priest in a quiet rural parish who suffers from panic attacks which come upon him suddenly and unexpectedly in various situations such as when he is shopping. He does not doubt his doctor's view that these attacks are caused by stress and realises that his anxiety that they might occur adds to his overall level of tension and increases the likelihood that they will. Yet he has no idea why he is stressed.

DENYING STRESS

Many of us hide our stress, sometimes so effectively we don't realise that we are stressed or why. In many professions, admitting to stress is taken as a sign that a person is not able to cope with the job. Certainly some organisations and individuals within them hold this view or don't take the problem of stress seriously. Even if this is not the case, we often fear that it is, and that our job is at risk. Some people fear that if they reveal they are stressed, it will be seen as an admission of weakness or failure, and they won't take advantage of stress-management programmes set up by their employers because they think this reflects badly on them. Many people therefore carry on until they suffer a physical or mental breakdown, or make costly or disastrous mistakes at work.

STRESS FACTORS

Meeting deadlines, speaking in public, noise, motorway driving, crowds, interviews, examinations and medical tests are commonly identified as stressful. You may think that everyone experiences them in much the same way, that it is 'normal' to be stressed by them, unavoidable and inevitable, but this is not so. Many people would find it extremely stressful to drink ten pints of fluid one after the other. Yet many people drink this amount of beer or lager in an evening and find it very pleasurable. Indeed they might be distressed if prevented from doing so. Similarly, some people find the idea of jumping from a bridge suspended only by a length of elastic quite horrifying, while others consider it fun. It therefore makes little sense to regard specific events and circumstances as stressful in themselves. Yet this is precisely what psychologists did when they adapted the concept of stress and applied it to human activities.

ASSESSING STRESS

Stress is interpreted by psychologists to mean the changes or adjustments made by the body to any demand placed on it. Accordingly any kind of change came to be seen as stressful irrespective of whether it was a change for the better, such as gaining a promotion at work, or for worse, such as being made redundant. The demands resulting from the rapid social and technological changes following the Second World War gave rise to increasing concern about the stress of modern life, and this led two psychologists in the 1960s to score the stress impact of life events on a scale of 0–100. They assigned the death of a spouse the maximum stress rating and included in their scale items such as divorce, moving house, holidays, giving up smoking, pre-menstrual tension and jet lag. It was their view that a person who scores highly on the scale as a result of having experienced a number of these events over the previous eighteen months is at risk of developing stress-related disease.[1] Subsequently many other scales and tables of stressful events were drawn up as a guide to the amount of stress a person can withstand.

It is now realised that this kind of formulation is much too simplistic and that the interaction between life events and an individual is considerably more complex. An unhappy marriage, unsatisfactory job or poor living conditions, while not events as such, may nevertheless be highly stressful. Moreover, not only life events but relatively mundane occurrences, irritations and hassles need to be taken into account, not only because major life events are frequently accompanied by minor concerns such as the car breaking down on the way to visit a sick relative in hospital, but also because in the short term these minor annoyances are known to be better predictors of stress-related conditions than are major life events. Moreover, these stress checklists typically exclude events that are often very stressful to some people, such as the illness of a pet animal, routine health screening, dealing with minor officials or workers in and around the home, or discovering a spider in the bath. More recently developed scales measuring stress levels score individual events on a ten-point scale and include items such as buying and selling a house, increasing a mortgage, having a child start at school, and pet-related problems. Nevertheless, assigning a fixed numerical stress rating to any event can be highly misleading.

The stress impact of an event, whether major or minor, may appear very different when viewed objectively than when it is experienced subjectively by an individual. For some people the death of a budgerigar can be more stressful than the death of a spouse. Indeed there are some people who admit it is the continued existence of their spouse that they find stressful. The impact of the same event will vary, often dramatically, from person to person. As the psychologist Gordon Allport once observed: 'The same fire that melts the butter hardens the egg.'

Individual differences in character — what might even be referred to in quasi-engineering terms as our 'metal' — determine the extent to which we react to stress. 'Hardy' types are known to withstand more and greater stress than 'softies' who succumb to it easily and break down more quickly.

Emphasis on stressful events implies that stress is beyond personal control and is therefore inevitable. This obscures the individual's role in determining stress. As we have seen, it is not events in themselves that are stressful but the way in which we perceive and interpret them. The stress associated with an event depends on how you view it, and this is largely a matter of attitude. If you view an event negatively, you will tend to experience it as unpleasant and try and avoid it. You are likely to cope with it less well than someone who views it positively, as an opportunity to learn, grow and develop, or simply as a novel experience to be relished. If your attitude is habitually negative, you are more likely to be continually stressed and to succumb to stress-related illness. If you generally view events positively, as a challenge rather than a threat, you are likely not only to cope with them without experiencing stress and becoming ill, but you may also thrive on them. Avoiding these situations might prove more hazardous and stressful for you if, as a result, you become inert, understimulated and bored. According to this scenario, you are not stressed by events beyond your control but by circumstances you create and then respond to stressfully. In effect you are stressing yourself. For this reason it is more useful to think in terms of particular *stressors* — those events and circumstances that you perceive as stressful — rather than *stress* in general.

IDENTIFYING STRESSORS

You might suppose that it is easy to identify the stressors in your life, and up to a point it is. We can usually identify some of the situations that we respond to in a stressful way. However, as noted above, we often do not realise we are stressed, and even if we do it isn't always possible to identify what triggered this response. This is because many stressors are unconscious — that is, usually we do not or cannot put them into words and so are unable to express them to ourselves or others. Nor can we think about them rationally and logically, so our stress reactions also appear irrational to us.

Many aspects of our experience are unconscious because we either don't have words for them or the words we do have are inadequate. We are obliged to describe virtually every positive emotion we experience in terms of either 'liking' or 'loving'.

There is very little in between. We can 'like' something or somebody a little or a lot, and love everything from cheeseburgers and chips to our mother and God. Without an adequate means of describing our emotions, it is sometimes difficult to identify them.

Other aspects of our experience are unconscious because we have repressed them. That is, we have excluded from conscious awareness — put out of our minds — potentially painful or dangerous thoughts and desires, which, if expressed, would be disapproved of and perhaps punished by others. We are usually not aware that we have repressed these thoughts, much less aware of why. To all intents and purposes, these aspects of ourselves are lost or hidden away. Nevertheless unconscious fears and anxieties about the reactions of others towards us and the constant need for their approval are a major source of stress for most people.

Given that these stressors are largely unconscious, it might appear that identifying them is impossible. Yet it isn't, as the following exercise shows.

EXERCISE FIVE

IDENTIFYING YOUR STRESSORS

Find somewhere you can sit or lie comfortably. Become aware of how your body is located in relation to its surroundings. Be aware of your feelings in this situation. How do you feel? Do you feel silly, or guilty about taking time to do the exercise? Do you feel impatient to get on with it? How self-conscious are you? Are you worried about being seen by others, or, if you are doing the exercise in company, are you anxious about their proximity, and the smells and sounds emitted by your body or theirs? Are you worried about falling asleep or snoring, or concerned that you might not be able to do the exercise? Your reactions may reflect some of the basic anxieties of your life, and relate to the tensions you habitually experience. If, during any part of the exercise, thoughts, feelings, memories or impressions come to mind, make a mental note of them as these also may provide a key to your underlying tensions.

Having identified how you feel, close your eyes or focus with open eyes on a fixed point or object. Then gradually withdraw your attention from your surroundings and direct it to your body and the surfaces adjacent to it. As you do so, notice whether the contact is uncomfortable or painful, and adjust your position so as to maximise comfort and minimise pain. You may feel that you need to remove restrictive clothing, shoes, spectacles or jewellery. At any point during the exercise when you feel the need to adjust your position, do so.

When you are positioned as comfortably as possible, bring your attention to your chest. Imagine there is a butterfly there that has just emerged from its cocoon and is slowly and progressively drying and stretching out its wings in the warmth of the sun. Breathe in and out deeply and with each in-breath imagine that you are breathing life and vitality into the butterfly and that it is spreading its wings more and more. Continue to breathe in and out deeply for some minutes, observing the butterfly carefully and also your reactions to it.

Imagine that the butterfly is preparing to take flight. It seems more and more likely to do so each time you breathe in and out deeply, but remains there for some time without doing so. At the point where the butterfly seems about to take flight, breathe out and observe what happens. Note your reactions when eventually it takes flight.

Now imagine following the butterfly to a pleasant location where you feel relaxed, at ease, comfortable and secure. Pay careful attention to the sights, sounds, smells and sensations of this place; how it feels and how you feel in it. Imagine all the details of the scene as vividly as possible, and take note of them. Allow yourself to enjoy being there and to relax as fully as possible.

Having done so, ask yourself what aspects of this imaginary situation you find particularly restful or relaxing. What features of everyday life are you getting away from here? If the answer isn't clear to you, compare the imaginary situation with the usual situations of your everyday life. What might this exercise tell you about the stressors in your life?

When you have answered these questions, allow yourself to spend a few minutes longer relaxing. Remember that this imaginary place is always there for you to go to. You carry it within yourself and can return there any time you choose.

Now allow the image to fade and prepare yourself to return your awareness to your surroundings. As you do this, take a few moments to orient yourself before recording the significant features of the exercise, including your answers to the above questions.

REACTIONS TO THE EXERCISE

Self-Consciousness

Your reactions, however trivial, to each aspect of the above exercise are potentially very revealing and can provide valuable insights into the mental stressors that create considerable tensions for you personally, although you are normally unaware of them.

Consciously Tom was 'more than ready for anything' when he began the exercise:

> 'So you can imagine my disappointment when I found myself incapable of sustaining my images. I could visualise the butterfly resting on my chest, rising and falling with my breathing, watch it fly off. . . . I found myself willing it so hard, all my concentration bent to achieving this end. Then, all of a sudden, I began wondering what I looked like sitting in this room, with my eyes closed, chasing butterflies; wondering also what the other people were thinking. Did they really have their eyes closed? Or were

they all sitting watching me? What are the others doing? Should I just open one eye and have a look? By this time, of course, any idea of relaxing, let alone following the butterfly, had gone out of the window.

'At this point I start to worry that I couldn't do the exercise. I tried not to panic. Maybe it's just this situation — a small room, pretty close to these people I don't know. I tell myself it shouldn't make any difference, but obviously it does. So what now? Solution: do it at home — nobody to see what you're doing, so no need to spend most of the time squinting out of one eye, wondering what other people are doing and thinking. Put the neuroses on hold and get on with it!'

However, when Tom tried the exercise at home he found it no easier. He couldn't get comfortable, and kept shifting about, removing and loosening various bits of clothing:

'I was just starting to drift a bit, when I realised I was looking for any excuse to stop, and as soon as I thought this, everything crumbled away. Maybe I am just a raving neurotic after all. I tell myself, "Calm down, take a deep breath. The whole idea of the exercise is to relax, not to tie yourself in knots. You're obviously not doing it right. There must be some logical reason why it doesn't seem to be working for you."'

There is a reason, and it is quite simply that Tom's logical mind is not relaxed or switched off. At the very moment this seems to be occurring, his mind leaps in with anxious thoughts about what he is doing, how it may appear to others, and such like. This is a very common defensive reaction to the unconscious fear most of us have about losing our mind and rational control, even temporarily. If we are out of control, even a tiny bit, we may act in ways that others would find unacceptable. Hence Tom's concern about being neurotic and about others watching him. The immediate effect of this inner tension is to make physical relaxation impossible.

Many people who try relaxation exercises in a group have similar concerns about appearing silly, stupid or mad. Steve, for example, admitted to becoming 'a little anxious and self-conscious — generally feeling vulnerable because of those around me'. This vulnerability arises because since childhood we have all learned, albeit not necessarily consciously, that silliness, stupidity and madness are unacceptable and are punishable in various ways. Even if we have not experienced these punishments ourselves, we all know of those who have. So many of us live in dread of being made to look a fool or to be thought crazy. The tension generated by this unconscious fear makes us uncomfortable when performing the exercise. Frequently we are grateful for distractions, for any excuse not to carry on with it.

Distractability

The very act of trying to relax provides us with plenty of distractions and excuses not to do so. Some people find that as they begin to relax they encounter a residual anxiety, often quite unspecific and of which they were formerly unaware, but sufficiently disturbing to prevent them sustaining the level of relaxation already achieved or of progressing further. This is because their habitual psychological and physical defences against anxiety and the feelings that provoke it are weakened. Rebecca's experience is not unusual:

'My feeling of tranquillity was marred by an inexplicable feeling of anxiety. I became acutely aware of being alone and vulnerable and this made me feel uncomfortable. This in itself was a valuable lesson because it made me aware that subconsciously I may be more vulnerable than I like to believe, but I also came to realise later that there is no need to feel so vulnerable and as a result I have subsequently been able to relax more fully.'

Some people experience a spontaneous release of emotion as certain muscles relax, and this can be very disconcerting. Sandra found herself crying for no obvious reason and only later realised that her tension protects her against feelings of hurt and sadness that might otherwise overwhelm her.

Sometimes the source of the anxiety is quite specific, as is the case with those people who cannot imagine a place where they would feel secure. Intrusive and unpleasant images may also arise which generate anxiety and tension and hence prevent relaxation. When examined more closely, such images invariably reveal the unconscious fears, anxieties, concerns or memories that produce tension and contribute to stress, and for this very reason we tend to defend ourselves by banishing them from our conscious minds.

Bodily sensations such as vibrations, waves, feelings of lightness or being suspended are commonly experienced when we begin to relax. Tingling or pins and needles in limbs or body parts, loss of sensation and odd feelings such as the arms appearing to be on the wrong way round or the hands being on different arms may also be experienced. These sensations may sometimes be alarming or feel unpleasant but they are entirely consistent with the physiological shifts that occur during relaxation and are a clear indication that the desired state is being achieved. Nevertheless, if you experience them, they may prevent you progressing further with the exercise. Chris felt he was unable to do so as he became dizzy and anxious and would fall off his chair, and Charlie was jolted out of his relaxed state when he 'felt' his right arm fall off as he imagined the butterfly taking flight. Both of them later admitted to anxiety about 'losing it' — 'it' being rational control as opposed to the tension it habitually generates in them. Alison also thought she was losing her mind when she imagined flying off on the back of an elephant, and this anxiety prevented her continuing with the exercise.

Censorship

If you find your imagination playing odd tricks like this — that is, producing unexpected imagery or that which you regard as unacceptable to yourself or others — you may be tempted to censor or change it. This kind of censorship is potentially very significant because it indicates the extent to which you act in accordance with what you think you *should* and *shouldn't* do. As we will see later, the *shoulds* and *should nots* that dominate people's lives often generate stress and stress-related illness.

Effort

Like Tom, many people who find it difficult to relax are simply trying too hard. Trying is in itself a stress or strain, whether we make an effort mentally or physically. Activities involving effort are, by definition, upsetting, difficult or annoying; they create tension. So the more you try, the less likely you are to achieve relaxation. However, you have probably been told from an early age that if you don't succeed at anything it is because you're not trying hard enough, and that you *should* try harder.

Tom's comments above reveal anxiety as to whether he is doing the exercise properly. This in itself is sufficient to inhibit relaxation because anxiety translates into muscular tension. It also illustrates the way in which concern about performance, achievement, success, failure or evaluation creates tension in our lives and limits our experience.

Eleanor only discovered, through attempting to relax, how anxious she is not to fail in anything she does. She is by no means alone; many of us live in fear of failure. It can prevent us attempting anything at all, so that we become inert. Indeed fear of failure is a well-recognised psychological syndrome. So too is fear of success. When Angela realised she had relaxed successfully, she became stressed:

'I realised that I can equally be stressed when I have no stressors in my life. I therefore have no real desire to escape from them.'

On the face of it, her assessment seems quite strange, yet it is a common experience to feel that one *should* have something to worry about, and that something is wrong if this is not the case. As Angela admits:

'It is not that I feel happy when I am stressed, but rather that this is what I am used to. There is a more relaxed, flowing and easygoing side of me struggling to get out but I don't feel it should at the present time.'

Role Expectations

Many women cannot allow themselves to relax because they feel that they *should* be looking after others and *should not* be indulging themselves. Men often feel that they *should* work around the clock to support others, *should* achieve promotion and high salaries and *should not* take time off for themselves; and young people of both sexes may feel that they *should* work to attain qualifications and *should not* enjoy themselves. Even if people give themselves permission to relax, these imperatives prevent them doing so effectively. So, for example, when Vivien imagined herself sitting in a beautiful pine forest thoroughly enjoying its delicious scent, she suddenly smelled burnt toast. This reminded her that she *should* be at home carrying out domestic chores rather than taking it easy, and she was immediately snapped out of her reverie by a sudden increase in tension.

Self-Restraint

However, those people who are able to imagine the butterfly often gain remarkable insights into themselves, even if they are unable to take the imagery further. Mary found that every time her butterfly tried to fly from her chest, she tried to catch it, until finally it broke up in her hands. Subsequently she acknowledged that she always loses those things she wants to hold on to in life by trying too hard, and this generates much tension and stress.

Many people realise that in trying to keep the butterfly 'close to their chest', they damage it and prevent it from being able to fly. This usually reflects their tendency not to express themselves or 'let themselves go', and to suffer accordingly through the tensions generated. Derek described holding his butterfly close to his chest so that no one can see its 'true colours'.

Some people experience a sense of panic when their butterfly is about to fly. Fear of loss, especially of control, may be a significant stressor for them, but they may also fear following their natural inclinations and impulses. Some butterflies flutter their wings and make gestures towards flying without actually doing so. Some fall to the ground. These images can indicate that such people want to be free but are in some way restricted or restrained, and crumple in the face of their own authenticity. Others find that despite their efforts the butterfly cannot fly. Jackie observed that her butterfly still had part of its cocoon attached to its wings. She took this as a sign that she needs to let go of something before she can express herself fully. Given the cocoon aspect of the image, this is possibly some aspect of her background or childhood but may also relate to other stages of her life, or the protection afforded by marriage, other relationships or jobs. Where the butterflies that fail to fly are large, this may give rise to feelings of sadness relating to the loss of considerable potential.

Powers and Potentials

Difficulties in experiencing a sense of 'realness' or authenticity may be revealed in the butterfly image. Many people are unable to breathe life into it, and it remains a lifeless, two-dimensional tattoo, silhouette, template, appliqué decoration or cardboard cut-out. Sometimes the butterfly is larger than life and may produce anxiety because of its sheer size, scope and potential. As such, it may represent people's fear of their own potential and power. As Marianne Williamson explains: 'Our deepest fear is not that we are inadequate. Our deepest fear is that we are powerful beyond measure. It is our light not our darkness that most frightens us.'[2]

Many of us daren't acknowledge our potential, simply because to do so requires us to act on it and this requires a change in the status quo. Gillian's image of the butterfly reflects this. It left her only to settle back on her chest and fold its wings. She interpreted this as an indication that she was already relaxed and contented but acknowledged later that it indicated complacency, which is a defence against change and the uncertainties and anxieties it brings.

Another reason why we don't acknowledge our potential is because we are aware of a strong prohibition in society against our doing so. We have learned that we should hide our light under a bushel and that to do otherwise — to shine or sparkle, to be brilliant, bright, or dazzling — is to invite the opprobrium and jealousy of others. As the actor Lee Marvin once observed: 'White knights shine too brightly on the battlefield. They soon get knocked off.'

For these reasons we often focus on our imperfections and weaknesses. Hence Diana was distressed to see that her butterfly had large black spots which she interpreted as blemishes on her character. She hated everything about it and wanted to rid herself of it, rather than follow it, but she could not. She realised that this image reflects her inability to accept herself as she is and also how deeply ingrained her negative attitudes are and the extent to which they create constant stress and anxiety in her life.

Self-Discovery

Many people find that they quite spontaneously follow the butterfly and in so doing not only gain valuable insights but possibly discover themselves in the process. This is not altogether surprising given that the Greek word for butterfly, *psyche*, also means 'self' or 'soul', and the butterfly is commonly and universally used as a symbol of the real, true or authentic self and to represent qualities such as transformation, metamorphosis, change and freedom.

The stressors people are freed from when they relax in the exercise often surprise them. Peter admits:

> 'Rationally I perceived my main stressors as deadlines, workload and money, yet as a result of this exercise I see that my true stressors are other people, family and friends, and their expectations of me.'

Michelle expresses a similar insight:

> 'The fact I was alone on a hill suggests to me that even with my closest loved ones I cannot feel completely relaxed. The hill is a chance to get away from everything and everyone. Since discovering it, I am able to go there to relax when things get a little out of hand and also when I am unable to sleep.'

Jane was surprised that she had to go away from everyone, including her parents and boyfriend, because of the emotional demands they make on her. Kerry imagined herself on a sandy beach:

> 'There was absolutely no one around and I felt an overwhelming sense of peace, tranquillity and isolation. This confused me for a while as I generally spend very little time alone, but when I thought about it more, I

realised that there always seem to be too many people around who demand too much from me. I rarely spend time with the people I really want to see and never seem able to find the time to be alone doing exactly what I want to do. Consequently the beach seemed like a sort of heaven to me; a haven where I could do exactly as I wished without anyone asking me where I was going, who with or for how long. This taught me that I certainly need to find the time to be on my own, spend more time with the people I want to rather than feeling obliged to visit others and meet their demands. It also taught me that there is nothing wrong with wanting to be alone sometimes and that I do not need to feel any guilt about this. I realise it will result in less stress and tension for me and that I will also be more tolerant and patient with others.'

Freedom

The aspect of the exercise that Tania found most revealing was that the trees in the natural paradise she imagined were entwined so that no person or thing could reach her. The barrier provided by the trees gave her a sense of freedom:

'Freedom to be who I wanted to be and a retreat away from the demands of others. It highlighted how imprisoned I sometimes feel by the demands others make on me, which is primarily a result of my inability to say "no" to their various requests. There are times when I simply do not want to give up my time and energy, yet do so none the less. If I do say "no", then I feel guilty because I think I should be fulfilling my role as a care giver.'

Linda was surprised to imagine herself seated on a horse:

'To me the horse represented freedom. I felt free from everything and everybody when I was riding it. At this moment in time I don't feel I have any freedom; I am constantly being reminded of my responsibilities. I feel that freedom is what I want right now when my life is so full of commitments and responsibilities.'

Demands on Our Time

The requirements of others, our commitments and responsibilities to them, emerge as stressors for most people. It is these that occupy our much of our time. Not surprisingly, demands on our time emerge again and again as a significant stressor for many people. Lack of it is the excuse most commonly given for not relaxing. Jill's butterfly led her to a meadow to relax but she didn't want to be there:

'I was under pressure for time and had a million things to do before lunch.'

Time pressure creates considerable stress, as Brenda relates:

'When I reflected on the exercise, I was astonished at how heavy and relaxed my body was. I simply did not want it to end. I felt a "glow of contentment". It was like the wave-like motion of the butterfly's wings which continued even after it had flown away. When I looked at the clock I was flabbergasted to find nearly half an hour had passed. I had lost track of time completely. Immediately I realised how stressed I am by time. I make a daily list of tasks to be performed, many of these insignificant things that could easily be put off. At the end of my list is usually the most pressing task. I feel I cannot tackle this unless everything else has been dealt with and is out of the way. Often, therefore, I run out of time before I get to the task that needs to be completed. Alternatively I feel too tired to attend to anything else.'

Invasive Thoughts

Thinking about such tasks occupies a good deal of our time. Richard admits that constantly dwelling upon what he should do 'muddles up' his head:

> 'I have trouble concentrating on one thing and I have trouble relaxing because I can't stop other thoughts from interrupting.'

The peace and serenity that Jane felt as she imagined lying by a stream on a warm summer's day was disrupted by

> 'big black flies buzzing about and landing on my legs. I can only think that the flies indicate how difficult I find it to escape from everyday stressors, and how hovering problems are never far from my mind.'

By performing the exercise some people realise, perhaps for the first time, that they create the problems of their lives just as Jane created the 'hovering' problems that plague her imagination. Claire found herself beside a river in glorious sunshine:

> 'I had managed to escape from cars, people and the general noise of urban life. As I lay down next to the river on the lush green grass, I became aware of a man and a dog. The dog was running free and barking, and though initially I felt pleased to see them, it annoyed me because I felt they were intruding on my personal sanctuary. In discussion afterwards, it was suggested that perhaps I am my own worst enemy, as I had allowed myself to become irritated by an image I had created. On reflection I feel that not only do I need to escape from what is around me but I also have to escape from the demands I allow others to put on me and those I impose on myself. It was only through this

image that I realised how irritated I am by the expectations my boyfriend has of my role in our relationship. I have since insisted on my own time to relax and study, and that everything comes second to that. I now realise that I allowed him to impinge on time which I need to spend on myself. He believes that as I don't work because I'm a student that I do nothing and so should have sole responsibility for running the house. I was surprised to learn that this is how I was feeling and at the intensity of my feelings. While I don't feel I am by any means a walkover, I now appreciate how easily resentment can build and that with resentment comes tension, stress and exhaustion. Allocating myself that time allows me to reflect on myself and to appreciate what I have achieved rather than what I have failed to achieve.'

Not surprisingly, when people realise that their everyday lives are a source of so many tensions, stresses and dissatisfactions, they often feel like Rob:

'I remember the feeling of dread as the exercise drew to a close and I realised I had to return to the real world!'

VISUALISATION AND SELF-AWARENESS

You may be wondering why a simple exercise like the one given above can provide not only insight into the attitudes, expectations, assumptions, thoughts and beliefs that underpin much stress but also reveal clues as to how you can alleviate and manage stress. The reason is that it involves visualisation — our ability to think in pictures or visual images rather than words. This ability to see 'in the mind's eye' tends to be obscured by our reliance on thinking in words, and many of us only become aware of it when the verbal chatter in our head is temporarily suspended or reduced. This occurs spontaneously in dreams, during fantasy, day dreaming and reverie, and can be brought about deliberately during procedures in which we relax and stop thinking in words.

SEEING SOLUTIONS TO PROBLEMS

The ability to think in pictures provides us with an important tool for acquiring and processing knowledge. It gives us, quite literally, a different way of looking at ourselves and our lives. When combined with verbal reasoning, it increases the flexibility of our thinking and enhances our mental capabilities. The ability to 'see' the nature of reality and solutions to problems in this way appears to be the key to all creativity and creative living.

Visualisation shares many features with visual perception, including the ways in which they are processed in the brain. The saying 'a picture is worth a thousand words' also applies to visual images, which present a great deal of complex information much more quickly than language does. Visual images also correspond in most respects to perceived or seen objects and can replace them in our minds. We can therefore often answer questions just as well when we merely imagine them as when we actually perceive them. We can also imagine all the perspectives which might be perceived when viewing objects from various sides and angles. We can further modify these images and obtain information from them just as we might do with corresponding physical objects and processes. We can mentally rotate imagined objects, add, subtract, superimpose or otherwise change their features and move them around in various ways. We can indeed 'turn things over' in our minds and so, as a means of reality testing and problem solving, thinking in images is often superior to rational, logical strategies that rely on verbal thinking. It is even possible to imagine specific activities without taking the time, making the effort or running the risk of carrying out those activities in physical reality. In this way we can often make startling discoveries, like Einstein who, by imagining himself travelling in space alongside a beam of light, developed his theory of relativity.

GAINING A DIFFERENT PERSPECTIVE ON TIME

Visualisation is in itself highly absorbing and, as with any activity that engages and occupies our attention, it is also relaxing. The manner in which images form simultaneously and instantaneously in the mind results in a sense of the passage of time that is quite unrelated to serial clock time. This relieves time-related stress in those for whom time is a pressure, and because it helps reduce reliance on verbal thinking, it relieves the physical tensions that frequently arise from mental anxieties.

REVERSING THE PHYSICAL EFFECTS OF STRESS

Creating mental images can also have direct physiological effects. It is well known that if we imagine eating a lemon our mouth begins to water and that sexual and phobic imagery can produce dramatic physiological reactions. It is less widely known but just as well established that visualisation can produce changes in blood flow, blood-sugar levels, blood pressure, perspiration, muscular tension, gastro-intestinal activity, breathing and immune function — that is, all the physiological processes adversely affected by stress. This suggests that visualisation may help us to control physiological functions formerly thought to be involuntary, and to harness this ability more systematically in the treatment of stress and stress-related illness.

GAINING ACCESS TO THE UNCONSCIOUS

Although the way in which visualisation works is still not precisely understood, it appears that the creation of mental images build a bridge between mind and body, allowing information to cross from the physical domain to the psychological, and vice versa. Physiological information may be perceived in visual or symbolic form as images. These can provide important clues to physiological functioning and be used as a tool for penetrating and exploring previously unconscious or hidden physiological and emotional processes.

Images may offer a more immediate and direct expression of the unconscious than language as they are less likely to be filtered through the conscious, rational process of censorship that words are subjected to before they assume grammatical order and can be spoken.

Visualisation is a valuable way to unlock and express issues that may be difficult for us to articulate — not only emotions and other feelings for which words may be inadequate but also issues that may have affected one personally such as sexual abuse, phobias, bullying, emotional and physical pain. It is particularly effective with children, for whom fantasy is very much 'first nature' and who may have difficulty expressing themselves adequately in words. Visualisation is used increasingly by social workers, educational psychologists and teachers. It can also give parents insight into the normally hidden realms of their children's experiences (their fears, anxieties, needs, wishes and preoccupations) and help them monitor their emotional and psychological needs more sensitively. Certainly, to the extent that visualisation helps us explore our inner worlds, it can help us to become more sensitive to the needs of others.

Within psychotherapy, visualisation has long been used to uncover and explore unconscious processes. It is a feature of many important psychotherapeutic approaches, including psychoanalysis, Jungian analysis, Gestalt therapy, psycho-synthesis, behaviour therapy, aversion therapy, arts and drama therapy. It is used to enhance feelings of control and the ability to cope in various situations, thereby reducing the fear of them; and to rehearse alternative strategies for dealing with such situations. It is also a source of detail about past experiences and can provide access to significant memories of early childhood before language became predominant. It can promote a richer experience of a range of emotions, bypass defences and resistances, and open up new avenues for exploration when therapy reaches an impasse.

GUIDING THE IMAGINATION

Therapists generally prefer to work with a person's spontaneously produced visual images. However, visualisation is often 'guided', as in the above exercise. The use of guided imagery can be likened to creating a movie in the mind whereby the subject, following a storyboard provided by another, casts, directs, produces, enacts, views and reviews a new imaginary experience that enables that person to confront the contents of his or her unconscious and relate these directly, and often dramatically, to personal circumstances and problems. The effectiveness of guided visualisation has led to its widespread use within psychotherapy and counselling, and visualisation directed towards personal growth, self-development, psychological and spiritual transformation, positive mental health and physical well-being is widely pursued as a powerful means of achieving self-awareness, self-help and stress relief.[3]

KEY POINTS

1. Stress originates in your mind — in the the way you see and think about yourself and the world — and in your imagination.

2. Much stress results from your worst imaginings, but its effects are nevertheless real.

3. You respond to threatening situations physiologically in ways that enable you to deal with them. If this state of high arousal is maintained over time or triggered repeatedly, it leads to wear and tear of your major bodily organs and to diseases related to hypertension, such as arteriosclerosis, coronary heart disease and stroke, cardiovascular disease, diabetes, brain damage, kidney failure and dysfunctions of the immune system.

4. You may be unaware that your body is stressed or of the circumstances producing this reaction.

5. This does not mean stress is beyond your control. It is not events in themselves that are stressful but the way in which

you perceive and interpret them. This is largely a matter of attitude.

6. If you generally view events negatively, as a threat, you are more likely to be stressed and to succumb to stress-related illnesses than if you generally view events positively, as a challenge. With a positive outlook you are more likely to cope with events without experiencing stress and becoming ill, and to thrive on the sense of challenge.

7. Much of the stress you experience is not triggered by events as such but by largely unconscious factors including the litany of directives — *shoulds* and *should nots* — you have learned and internalised throughout life. Once you have identified these stress factors or stressors, you can rid yourself of many of them and cope more effectively with those you cannot eliminate.

8. Visualisation is a powerful means of gaining insight into these stressors and learning how to deal with them.

Becoming a More Balanced Individual

If you tighten the strings too much, they will snap,
and if you leave them too slack they won't play, but if they
are tuned to the right point, then, and only then does the
music start.

Siddhartha Gautama

STRESS AVOIDANCE

There is now little doubt that stress contributes to a great deal of illness, both physical and psychological, and it has become fashionable to think of stress itself as the major disease of the late twentieth century. The view of stress most widely promoted in recent years — and favoured, if we are honest, by most of us because it absolves us from any responsibility for the stress we suffer — is that stress is caused by external factors beyond our control and so must be avoided. Stress has therefore become a negative concept and stress avoidance the goal of many people pursuing health and happiness.

Avoiding Stressors

Having identified your personal stressors, you may think that the best way to deal with them is to avoid them all: your boss, work colleagues, bank manager, dentist, family, friends, neighbours, debtors, deadlines, exams, computers, the telephone, crowds, traffic, noise, pollution, even the cold and rain — anyone or anything that makes demands on you. Clearly this isn't a very realistic possibility, and so stress may seem unavoidable and inevitable.

Nevertheless, you may harbour fantasies that by retiring or giving up your job; moving from a city or town to live in the countryside or by the sea; going to live on a remote island or in another country, you could live a stress-free existence. However, even if you find your Shangri-La, you may discover that it doesn't quite live up to expectations.

Eileen found her real-life paradise in a tiny, undeveloped Greek island. She was very surprised to learn that most of its inhabitants spend only four or five months of the year there and 'escape' to a much larger and more developed island for the remainder. But as Costas, one of the islanders, explained after she had extolled the virtues of his homeland to him: 'Yes, it is sunny and warm and quiet. Tomorrow it will be sunny and warm and quiet. The day after it will be sunny and warm and quiet. Everyday it is sunny and warm and quiet, and we want something more than sun and warmth and quiet.'

You may have discovered or rediscovered a 'paradise', haven, idyll or retreat while you were performing Exercise Five (see Chapter Three). If so, try the following exercise and observe your reactions to it.

EXERCISE SIX

Revisiting Paradise

Find somewhere to sit or lie comfortably and take a few minutes to relax in whatever way seems most effective for you. Having done so, imagine returning to the place where the butterfly led you in the previous exercise — somewhere you can feel completely relaxed, at ease, comfortable and secure. Pay careful attention to the sights, sounds, smells and sensations of the place; how it feels and how you feel in it. Allow yourself to enjoy being there and to relax as fully as possible. Then imagine that you remain in that place all day; and the next day; and the next day . . . and so on. Identify your responses and make a mental note of the thoughts, feelings, impressions and sensations that arise. When you have done this, allow yourself to return your awareness to your ordinary surroundings, and reflect on the experience.

BLISS OR BOREDOM?

You may be able to identify your responses without even attempting the exercise. You may remember only too clearly returning to spend all day on the beach because you enjoyed it so much the day before; or to the wonderfully relaxing holiday resort you visited on a previous occasion. If so, you will know that you can only take so much bliss before you get bored. Most of us begin to 'die' of boredom very quickly, especially in the absence of other people, which is why solitary confinement is such torture. It is precisely the people and things we enjoy a reprieve from so much that we begin to miss and yearn for. As a result we often can't wait to get back to the very things we couldn't wait to get away from — our stressors.

The tendency to emphasise the undesirable and unhealthy aspect of stressors obscures the fact that they frequently serve a positive function in stimulating us and spurring us on to achievement and self-fulfilment. We need change and challenge, and most of us seek novelty and stimulation. The idea that we are passive victims of stress doesn't really make sense. If we really wanted to avoid stress completely, we would never study or learn anything new, never marry, have children or pets, go to work or travel. We would probably never leave the house.

However, we often need to be reminded that the demands made on us keep us on our toes and provide novelty and stimulus in our lives. The challenges in our lives can be exhilarating and exciting, giving us meaning and purpose. As such they can be desirable and healthy. So it is nonsense to suppose that stress is all bad and harmful. If we avoided our stressors entirely, we would probably become totally inert, which may ultimately prove more stressful and hazardous.

TOO MUCH OR TOO LITTLE STIMULATION

The brain appears to need a certain amount of stimulation and information to maintain its organisation. When there is too little or too much, instability results and disease may follow. Too much information and stimulation can destabilise the brain and result in what is now referred to as Information Fatigue Syndrome.

This new malaise was first identified in an international research report issued in 1996 and based on a survey of 1,313 junior, middle and senior managers in the UK, US, Australia, Hong Kong and Singapore. It points to the potentially serious consequences of information overload — stress, ill-health and poor quality of life — and makes it clear that finding ways of dealing with the ever-growing burden of information is now one of the most urgent challenges facing business worldwide. The report claims that information overload makes many managers mentally and physically ill, interferes with good decision-making, wastes time and impedes the progress of business and industry. Two thirds of the managers studied attributed tension with work colleagues and loss of job satisfaction to the stress associated with information overload, and almost as many believed their personal relationships had suffered as a result of it. British women were identified as particularly vulnerable to stress of this kind. A third of the managers claimed they suffer ill-health as a result of stress caused by trying to digest too much information.[1]

The main reason given for the ever-increasing quantity of information is the growth of communication. If you have ever returned home after a few days' absence and found you could hardly open your door for the great drift of newspapers, magazines, unsolicited mail, circulars and promotional literature, you will know that we are increasingly in danger of being buried under a mountain of information — much of it quite irrelevant to our needs or interests. The only way we can process it is by consigning most of it to the waste bin. As for 'surfing' the Internet, most of us are floundering out of our depth in floods of information.

Minette Marrin suggests that information fatigue is part of a more profound and pervasive sense of 'choice fatigue', and that we are spoilt *by* choice, not *for* it. She claims that we are deluged with information because we think we need it to make choices, when, for example, we are presented with thirty-seven different kinds of shampoo and forty-seven corresponding conditioners in a supermarket. She argues that what we need is less communication, less information and less choice — not more.[2]

On the other hand, destabilisation can result when the brain is understimulated. Understimulation resulting from sensory deprivation can cause the central nervous system to go awry and produce mental and physical disorders. For this reason it may be as damaging to the brain to be bored senseless as it is to be bombarded with information. We don't need sophisticated scientific research to tell us what we all know: boredom is itself stressful. It generates tension and anxiety. When we are bored, time weighs heavily on us, and bored people, when they are able to, often 'kill' time by taking drugs and alcohol, or otherwise distract themselves by eating, watching television or socialising. Boredom itself is often experienced as pain; it can literally be agonising.

THE IMPORTANCE OF MAINTAINING A BALANCE
The idea that stress is caused by too much or too little

stimulation is an oversimplification. The brain is constantly attempting to achieve a balance between information and experience, so it regulates the amount of stimulation, information and change that is optimal for the organism it controls. However, the stable level of stimulation or 'set point' it tries to maintain varies from one person to another, and may also alter throughout life as our needs for stimulation and information change. So, while we differ in the amount of stimulation we require, we nevertheless need to achieve what is an appropriate balance for each of us.

Stress is a symptom of inner and personal imbalance or disharmony. The degree to which we suffer from it says more about ourselves than the circumstances of our lives; more about how we live with ourselves than how we cope in the world. Dealing with stress in the long term requires us to strive towards and achieve inner balance rather than avoiding altogether the stressors in our lives. It involves knowing ourselves and our needs. We cannot control what we do not know or understand, and until we have looked closely into ourselves, we cannot hope to either, much less understand others. The difficulty in finding and maintaining the proper balance is that what we need is usually obscured by what other people want of and from us, and we have been conditioned to pay attention to them rather than to ourselves.

IDLE CHATTER

One of the dangers of becoming bored is that our minds seize on anything to occupy them in order to avoid seizing up. If we cannot provide them with some external stimulus, our minds will turn to its internal store of familiar messages, replaying them rather like the public address system in a 1950s-style holiday camp or a jukebox full of old records. So, although we may be relaxing in some idyllic spot and emptying our mind of its usual thoughts, anxieties and concerns, these will return as soon as our verbal thinking resumes. The messages on what can be thought of as our 'mind tapes' or 'mental records' — our own personalised communications or memos — comprise everything we've ever been told by others, and therefore the demands made on us, the *shoulds* and *should nots* that provide the usual commentary on our existence and that emerged as the most significant stressors in Exercise Five.

However, it is not only when we are bored that intrusive and recurrent thoughts arise. They tend also to occur whenever our minds are not otherwise preoccupied and set up patterns of stress, anxiety and tension. We tend to feel guilty if we haven't acted upon these directives and anxious about the consequences of not having done so. We may find ourselves engaged in worry cycles as we play over and over again in our minds, almost involuntarily, the same thoughts and anxieties.

If you sit for a while and notice the chattering in your head, you will find that you are carrying on many different inner conversations with yourself, and fragments of conversation, which you would think crazy if you overheard someone else saying them out loud. You may be telling yourself what you *should* have told someone else when they imposed on you, or what you *would* have told them if you had the courage to. You may be reviewing or rehearsing an entire repertoire of behaviour or dialogue, or planning your appearance and presentation. You may be telling yourself what you *would* or *should* be doing if you weren't doing what you are doing, and what you *must* do in future. You may be reminding yourself of what you could or should have done or did do in the past. You may be asking yourself questions: why you did what you did, why you think what you think, feel what you feel. You are probably either focusing your attention on your past or your future, and as a result you are not attending to the present. You are missing it. Our constant mental chattering literally robs us of life by preventing us noticing, much less enjoying, what each moment of life holds for us.

Don Juan Matus, the sage whose teachings are the basis for

the books of Carlos Castaneda, observes that we maintain our world with our internal talk: 'Not only that, but we also choose our paths as we talk to ourselves. Thus we repeat the same choices over and over until the day we die, because we keep on repeating the same internal talk over and over until the day we die.'[3]

What can we do about this relentless chatter? You may long for an answer, especially if it prevents you sleeping or concentrating on the important issues in your life. You may crave a set of mental windscreen wipers that will remove these intrusive thoughts and allow you to see things more clearly. Even if we successfully distance ourselves from our primary stressors — other people — we still retain the demanding messages we have been receiving from them throughout our lives and will continue to be stressed by these.

This was highlighted for me during the summer of 1995, one of the longest and hottest ever recorded in Britain. My husband, David, and I had often said that if we could guarantee good weather we would much prefer to spend our summer holiday at home, enjoying the beautiful Shropshire countryside in which we live than travel abroad, but we had arranged to drive to Tuscany and stay in a village where we had previously enjoyed a wonderful holiday. We had eagerly looked forward all year to our vacation but on the eve of our departure we were reluctant to leave the British heatwave. However, as David reminded me, our ferry crossing and hotel en route had been booked and paid for, our hotel room in Tuscany reserved, and the car was packed. We agreed that it would be madness to abandon the holiday now. So, in the early hours of the following morning, we set off. By the time we reached our hotel near the Swiss border that evening, it had been raining for several hours. It continued to rain overnight and the next morning as we headed towards Switzerland it was still raining heavily.

After some time spent driving in silence, I asked David whether he really wanted to go to Tuscany. 'Of course,' he replied, but some two hundred yards further down the road, he stopped the car and asked me whether I still wanted to go. I said I wasn't sure but I didn't think I did. He admitted he wasn't too sure himself. We sat and deliberated for some minutes. Of course we should go, we reasoned. We would be mad not to. It would be hot in Tuscany and we should be able to relax and enjoy ourselves as we had done before. So we continued. After another few hundred yards, David stopped the car again. He'd been thinking about it and he really wasn't at all sure he wanted to go on. By this time we were both totally confused. We weren't sure what we felt individually or to what extent our decision to continue had been based on what we thought each other actually wanted to do. As we tried to unravel the issues we were both wrestling with, the rain continued to pour down. Eventually and rather uncertainly, we turned the car in the direction of home, but after a few hundred yards stopped once again for another case conference. Were we doing the right thing? We agreed that it felt right and that we had only proceeded with the trip because we thought we *should*. We both felt a sense of relief at having decided to go home. Once we recognised this we continued homewards, and for two hours recited a litany of the *shoulds* that influence every aspect of our lives and obscure what we really think, feel, need and want. It was as hilarious as it was alarming.

The rain stopped as we neared Calais. Back in Shropshire the next day, the heatwave continued. Everyone we met responded in exactly the same way. They all said we must be mad, but that they admired us for acting on our feelings. Several added that they knew they couldn't have done so. We never regretted our decision for a moment and spent a blissful fortnight doing what we had always wanted to do. If we had ignored our feelings and done as we thought we should, we would have missed a memorable experience. Of course it could have been quite different, but it wasn't.

BEING SINGLE-MINDED

Even though David and I were many miles distant from the significant people in our lives, and travelling alone, it was not easy for us to distinguish what we wanted from our lives from other people's ideas, expectations, reactions, assumptions and requirements of us; and the already hazy picture was further obscured by each of us thinking we *should not* disappoint or let down the other.

In order to meet our needs and avoid stress, each of us needs to distance ourself psychologically rather than physically from others. The most effective way to do this is by putting a distance between ourselves and the messages we habitually repeat to ourselves. You might think this rather strange given that these messages are in our heads. Distancing ourselves from this chatter is not simply a matter of putting it from our minds because, as we've seen, as soon as we empty our minds or suspend the immediate thoughts that have been keeping familiar, intrusive thoughts at bay, the chatter resumes. Nor is it a matter 'getting out of your head', so much as becoming single-minded. This is because we are nearly always in two minds.

Our brain is divided into two halves or hemispheres. The left hemisphere is primarily responsible for the production of language and verbal thinking, whereas the right hemisphere controls non-verbal processes, including the autonomic nervous system, the immune system, pattern recognition, spatial awareness, perception and imagination. The left hemisphere thinks primarily in words whereas the right thinks in images. The former tends to dominate our thinking because our culture highly values verbal thinking and communication, which distinguish us as a species from other animals, characterise our evolution and underpin our scientific and technological progress. The left hemisphere also has the advantage of having a voice, whereas the right hemisphere remains silent.

The only time most of us become aware that we think in images is when the verbal chatter in our heads is turned off or down. This occurs when we are asleep, in the form of dreams and during waking consciousness when we engage in fantasy, day dreaming or reverie. Common to all these states is relaxation. As we have seen, it is only possible to relax fully when our usual mode of verbal thought is suspended. When this occurs, images, notably visual images, spring to mind and often provide insights into features of ourselves and of our world of which ordinarily we are unconscious. This process also works in reverse, for by reducing the volume of mental chatter in our heads, we can relax.

Ordinarily, as we have seen, the chattering left hemisphere of our brain dominates our waking lives and by doing so produces stress. When stressed, the sympathetic branch of the autonomic nervous system (ANS) — which regulates automatic or involuntary functions such as blood pressure, heart rate and suchlike — has precedence over the parasympathetic branch of the ANS. When we relax, the parasympathetic branch of the ANS — concerned with rest and regeneration rather than action — is dominant. Its effects are therefore the opposite of the sympathetic branch of the ANS: it slows our heart beat, reduces the flow of air into the lungs, stimulates the digestive system and helps relax muscles. It predominates during sleep and also when we are day dreaming and fantasising.

Much as we might like to, we cannot exist permanently in the Never Never Land of dreams and fantasy, simply because we would never achieve anything. It is one thing to build a castle in the sky but quite another to try and live in it. Clearly a balance between these two modes of functioning is necessary if we are to avoid the dangers of either extreme.

We can achieve better balance both physiologically and psychologically if we become more single-minded. This involves turning down the volume of the mental chatter so as to increase parity and harmony between the functions of the left and right sides of the brain. This 'rights' the usual imbalance in our way of thinking by shifting the emphasis away from verbal processes. The new frame of reference that results enables us to gain a different perspective on and insight into many issues, including ourselves. Furthermore, the 'mind' that emerges from such a singular focus, and that we come to know, is our own authentic way of thinking rather than the 'collective' mind imposed by others. The most effective way of becoming more single-minded is via meditation, hypnosis, the Relaxation Response, Autogenic Training, creative visualisation and guided imagery, and looking at your dreams.

MEDITATION

We cannot switch off the chattering mind totally, but through meditation the chattering can be toned down and eventually made to disappear. There are hundreds of different ways to meditate but whatever the method the fundamentals remain the same: relaxation, watchfulness and a non-judgmental attitude. Rather than concentrating the mind, as is commonly supposed, meditation involves relaxing it, without any attempt to take control, and watching in a relaxed state of awareness whatever is going on, without interfering.

Thus the key to meditation is *witnessing*. This is a simple but profound state of watching and accepting ourselves as we truly are, silently observing the traffic of the mind — passing thoughts, desires, memories, dreams, images, fantasies — without judgment, evaluation or condemnation; saying neither 'this is good' nor 'this is bad'.

Meditation has no specific content but is simply attending and listening to inner experience; becoming more open to and aware of oneself. It is nothing but a device to make you more self-aware.

The Effects of Meditation

It is well known that meditation has a variety of beneficial effects. It is profoundly relaxing because it is not only a state of inaction or non-doing but also a complete letting go or abandonment of all notions about the self, or ego, and its limitations; of all ideals and beliefs about what one is or should be, and relaxing into what one is. It involves a gradual relinquishing of mental attitudes, preoccupations and concerns. As a result it reduces anxiety, and meditators are less anxious and enjoy better psychological health than non-meditators. There is some evidence that meditation is more effective than other relaxation techniques in bringing about changes in those experiencing habitual anxiety.[4] Regular meditators also report increased psychological stability, more positive mood states and a sense of being more in control and effective in the world rather than passive victims of circumstance. Meditation is also associated with psychological benefits such as a greater sense of self-fulfilment, improved sleep, decreased drug use, reduced fears and phobias and a general state of positive mental health.

Meditation produces a pattern of observable physiological changes that is opposite to the flight or fight arousal response that, as we have seen, mobilises a set of physiological responses marked by increased blood pressure, heart rate, blood flow, oxygen consumption and muscle tension. Rather it generates an integrated response, or hypometabolic state — a state of balance or equilibrium characterised by quiescence rather than hyperactivity. Advanced practitioners can also voluntarily regulate normally autonomic or involuntary functions such as metabolic rate.

Advocates of meditation claim that regular practice over a period of time produces an overall quietening of the mind which transfers into ordinary waking consciousness and produces calmness and tranquillity. These claims are well supported by research, which reveals that through regular meditation it is possible to develop a habitually low state of arousal[5] and to derive long-term health benefits.[6] Meditation has been shown to create changes in the electrical activity in the brain, slow respiratory and heart rate, and lower blood pressure — all suggestive of deep relaxation. Those who regularly practise meditation (once or twice daily) can achieve and maintain reduced hypertension, greater physiological stability and a lower incidence of somatic complaints, headaches, colds and insomnia. They also report a reduction in their consumption of alcohol, cigarettes, caffeine and other drugs, and positive dietary changes. Recognition of its therapeutic benefits has led to increasing use of meditation in the treatment of stress and stress-related conditions.

How to Begin Meditation

Exactly the same process is followed in preparing for meditation as in relaxation. Find somewhere quiet where you can sit comfortably. It is preferable to sit as you are likely to fall asleep if you lie down, and while sleep is beneficial it is a different physiological state from meditation and confers different benefits. It is also advisable not to meditate immediately after a meal.

Sit with your body well supported along the length of your spine and by your legs. If sitting on a chair, ensure that your buttocks and thighs are firmly supported by the seat of the chair and that your feet are flat on the ground and apart. Rest your hands loosely on your thighs and make sure no parts of your body, including your hands, are twisted or clasped together. Imagine you are sitting so that your energy can flow unimpeded throughout your body from head to foot.

When you have done this, withdraw your attention from your surroundings and either close your eyes or focus them on a fixed point or object. This may be a mark on a wall or the floor, the flame of a candle or fire, a flower or other object. Assume a passive, non-judgmental attitude and witness what occurs. You may find it helpful to repeat silently to yourself the word *one* each time you breathe out as this will occupy the chattering part of your brain, which is likely to distract you. If and when it does, simply observe this and gently turn your mind back to passive witnessing. Accept whatever occurs as it occurs. If you don't feel relaxed, accept that this is so. Accept whatever thoughts arise, without censoring them, but do not hold on to them. Let them go. Allow yourself to continue doing so for approximately twenty minutes. Glancing at your watch or a clock once or twice will not impede the process of your meditation, and with regular practice you will find that you know when twenty minutes have passed. Give yourself a moment or two to readjust to your surroundings before continuing with your other activities.

HYPNOSIS

Hypnosis quietens the verbal chatter in our heads by occupying the left hemisphere of the brain with a specific stimulus such as counting backwards or some other mathematical or verbal formula. With the left side of our brain thus preoccupied, we can relax and the right hemisphere can function without the usual verbal interference. In this way constraints normally imposed on the mind by rational, conscious mental processes are relaxed and we can become aware of ordinarily unconscious features of ourselves — those features of which we are usually unaware — thereby enhancing self-awareness and enabling us to influence directly physiological processes normally beyond our control. In this way we may gain control of processes considered to be autonomic or involuntary. As with meditation, through hypnosis we can reduce blood pressure, heart and respiratory rate, and regulate other functions adversely affected by stress. Remarkable feats of strength and endurance normally considered impossible can also be achieved when 'conscious' control of bodily processes is suspended or removed, and under such conditions other effects are possible, including pain relief and anaesthesia during medical operations, and organic changes brought about, such as making warts disappear. We can also gain important insights into the sources of stress — our anxieties, fears, concerns and expectations — and also into our own hopes, needs, values and aspirations.

The Benefits of Hypnosis

The value of hypnosis as a means of reaching the repressed unconscious factors underpinning stress has long been recognised and its use in therapy, or hypnotherapy, is now widely promoted. Hypnosis has proved effective in the treatment of anxiety and phobic reactions, and stress-related disorders such as hypertension, asthma, migraine, eczema, backache, bedwetting and insomnia; in the treatment of repetitive cycles of behaviour such as addictions, smoking, over-eating and obsessive-compulsive reactions; and depression.

Some indication of the control of autonomic functions possible under hypnosis can be gained from the fact that many hundreds of operations have been performed with hypnosis as the sole anaesthetic. Hypnosis has been widely used in obstetrics and in operations such as appendectomy, caesarian section, breast surgery, skingrafting, heart surgery, cataract removal, prostrate resection, haemorrhoidectomy, nerve restoration and the ligation and stripping of veins. Hypnosis has also proved to be a valuable painkiller. Indeed studies have found that hypnosis is more effective than acupuncture, Valium, aspirin and placebos in relieving experimentally induced pain, and that its effects are more or less equivalent with morphine.[7] Hypnosis has also been used in the treatment of cancer to control pain, anxiety and insomnia. It has been found to help restore the sense of self-control that is often lost during the course of treatment of invasive cancer and to overcome the vomiting and nausea associated with chemotherapy, which is commonly resistant to anti-emetic drugs. Its role in improving immune function has also been demonstrated.

Hypnosis is an effective means of listening to the inner self. Although widely misrepresented and misunderstood, it achieves its effects primarily by helping us to relax or let go of the constraints we normally impose on our minds and bodies by rational, conscious mental processes — the scripts we have internalised throughout life. Hypnosis exploits one of the fundamental tenets of these scripts, our belief in the authority and expertise of others — in this case the hypnotist — and our willingness to comply with his or her suggestions. However, these effects are directed not towards a loss of control, as is commonly supposed, but towards the loosening of the rigid control our conscious mind normally exerts over our being by way of its scripts. So we are not in any sense handing control over to the hypnotist but, on the contrary, gaining greater self-control of our functions. Hypnosis can therefore be more properly thought of as guided self-hypnosis, and as such it is highly appropriate to the process of self-actualisation.

Hypnotic induction is in most respects similar to relaxation procedures. It usually commences with you sitting or lying comfortably and having your visual concentration trapped and held by focusing on a fixed point or object. This strains the eye muscles and quickly induces sensations of heaviness in the eyelids and their closure, which may be encouraged by suggestions of heaviness. When your eyes are closed, relaxation is achieved through attention to your breathing and the release of tension in various parts of your body. This may be augmented by counting backwards or by performing an imaginary activity such as descending steps. You are then encouraged to imagine a relaxing scene as vividly as possible, and when deep relaxation is achieved, positive affirmations or suggestions relevant to a desired objective may be introduced.

How to Hypnotise Yourself

Lying or sitting comfortably, either close your eyes or focus them on a fixed point or object, and begin silently counting backwards from three hundred. If you are distracted, simply return your attention to counting downwards.

Imagine that you are descending some steps, matching your breathing with each step and on each one progressively releasing a little more of the tension in the muscles of your body so that you become more and more relaxed. Imagine that it is a warm, sunny day and you are descending the steep stone steps of a high sea wall on to a beach. As you descend these steps, you pause on each one to take a deep breath. As you do so, you can smell the sea and taste the salt in the air. With each step you feel warmer and warmer, and your limbs feel more and more heavy. You pause on each step. You can see an empty expanse of sand beneath you, extending towards the sea. There are no people, only a few gulls and wading birds. This pleases you and you remain for a few moments on each step enjoying the solitude and warmth, the sights, sounds, smells and sensations of this unspoilt place. When you reach the bottom of the steps, you find that the heat reflected from the sea wall makes you warmer still, and as you step into the sand, your legs feel heavy. Your feet sink deeply into the fine, warm sand and walking is an effort. The feeling of heaviness in your legs spreads throughout your body as you walk across the sand towards the sea and you feel progressively tireder and long to lie on the sand.

When you get within a few metres of the sea, you lie down, spreading yourself on the sand. Immediately you feel the warmth from the sand below and from the sun above. As you sink into the sand, you feel comfortable and relaxed. The tensions in your body melt away as you lie looking upwards at the cloudless blue sky. Your eyes begin to close and as they do you become more aware of the smell of the sea, and you inhale deeply several times. You can taste salt on your lips and feel a fine spray on your body. You can hear the waves breaking gently on the sand, and each time you hear the inward rush of water, you count *one*. Gradually your mind empties of thoughts, preoccupations and concerns, leaving you relaxed in mind and body, feeling tranquil and at ease, in harmony within yourself and with your surroundings.

Allow yourself time to enjoy this experience, and then, feeling fully revitalised and energetic, open your eyes and stand up. Walk briskly, easily and effortlessly towards the sea wall. Finding the steps there, ascend them quickly, counting them as you go. When you reach the top of the sea wall, pause briefly to take a last look at the sea. As you do so, the image of the sea fades. Your awareness gradually returns to your surroundings and you open your eyes.

THE RELAXATION RESPONSE

US heart specialist Professor Herbert Benson insists that relaxation is not a skill but an inborn response we are all capable of achieving, although most of us have forgotten how to. He has developed a method for eliciting what he terms the Relaxation Response, which combines elements of both meditation and hypnosis in as much as it provides a very simple formula to occupy the left hemisphere of the brain thereby enabling the mind and body to relax effectively.

Benson suggests that you simply repeat the word *one* on each outbreath while sitting in a quiet place with your eyes closed. Whenever your mind wanders or you are disturbed by a sound or thought, simply return your mind gently back to repeating the word again, and continue to do so for 15–20 minutes.

His technique focuses primarily on improving the efficiency of breathing. This is important because it provides the oxygen necessary to release energy from food and deliver it to your muscles, and so by increasing your oxygen intake you make more energy available. By focusing on breathing, Benson's method diverts your mind from its habitual preoccupations, enabling relaxation to occur progressively as mental tensions are relinquished. Relaxation is enhanced further by being encouraged to visualise a pleasant scene.[8]

During the Relaxation Response physiological changes occur that are similar to those achieved by way of meditation, and this method has proved effective in the treatment of hypertension, headache and many other stress-related conditions, including addictions and drug abuse. In many US hospitals it is used as a standard pre-operative procedure and is routinely employed in the treatment of cardiovascular disease. It is effective in the control of chronic pain, asthma, the regression of cancer and in reducing the side-effects of chemotherapy for cancer. It can improve immune response, reduce a diabetic's need for insulin and relieve conditions associated with anxiety.

AUTOGENIC TRAINING

During the 1930s the German neurologist and psychiatrist Johannes Schultz used insights derived from his observations of hypnosis in developing the self-help system of relaxation known as Autogenic Training. He noted that hypnotised subjects generally report two characteristic sensations — a pleasurable feeling of warmth in their limbs and torso and a sensation of heaviness. Both are in fact physiological correlates of relaxation: the feeling of warmth is the subjective perception of vasodilation in the peripheral arteries; and the sensation of heaviness is the subjective perception of muscular relaxation. Schultz concluded that if he could design exercises which would enable subjects to induce these sensations in themselves, he might be able to teach them how to achieve the passive concentration, or 'witnessing', which is a feature of both hypnosis and meditation, and which, once achieved, enables greater control of bodily and mental functions.

So Schultz devised various verbal stimuli to occupy the left hemisphere of the brain, but unlike other methods the formulae he used were specific suggestions embodying physiological sensations such as 'My right arm is heavy', 'My right arm is warm'. These suggestions are repeated several times, alternating with a cancellation formula — 'Arms firm, breathe deeply, open eyes' — and vigorous movements of the limbs. By gradually training the body/mind complex in this way over a period of 2–12 months, complete relaxation can eventually be achieved in a matter of 2–4 minutes.

Autogenic Training has been subjected to considerable clinical research and it is clear that significant reductions in blood pressure, respiratory and heart rates can be achieved.

Indeed Schultz claimed that hypertensive patients could achieve a reduction of 10–20 per cent in their blood pressure. Other physiological effects, such as pain relief, can be induced by Autogenic Training, which has also been used effectively in treating a wide range of stress-related illnesses, and integrated into the medical training programmes of many European and US universities.

Autogenic Procedure

Schultz believed that anyone can achieve deep relaxation through Autogenic Training, providing he or she is motivated to do so. He recommended that external stimulation is reduced to a minimum, restrictive clothing, jewellery and spectacles removed, and three basic postures adopted: horizontal, reclining in an armchair or sitting upright.

The horizontal posture requires you to lie on a bed, couch or floor, legs slightly apart, feet inclined outwards at a V-shaped angle, and with support under the knees to provide maximum relaxation of the leg muscles. Position your head carefully and comfortably, without stiffness in the neck or cramped shoulders. Allow your arms to lie relaxed and slightly bent, with the fingers of your hands spread and relaxed and not touching the main part of your body. In its resting position your body should be corpse-like, without muscle tension. (This posture is virtually identical to the *sarasana* or 'corpse' posture of hatha yoga, which has a significant effect in relaxing the body.)

The reclining and sitting postures not only help to prevent you falling asleep but are also useful if you wish to practise the exercises in a more public setting such as the office. If you choose to recline in an armchair, ideally it needs a high back and a seat equal to the length of your thighs so that the small of your back rests easily against the back of the chair. Rest your hands, fingers outstretched, on the arms of the chair or allow them to hang loosely at your sides. If you use a straight-backed chair, sit on the edge so that only your buttocks rest on the seat with the thighs touching it only slightly. Position your feet one in front of the other so that the heel of one foot is in direct alignment with the toes of the other. This will support your lower trunk.

Once you have achieved one of these basic postures, imagine that a string attached to the top of your head is pulling you into an upright position with both your arms hanging by your side. Then imagine that the string is cut so that your head flops like a rag doll. Ensure that your body doesn't collapse into a concave posture so that breathing becomes difficult, and allow your arms to swing upwards so that your hands and fingers hang loosely between the knees without touching. In this relaxed position you can begin the first, or standard, series of exercises.

Stage One

Direct your attention to whichever arm seems most active and repeat silently to yourself the instruction 'My right/left arm is heavy' 3–6 times for 30–60 seconds. Then flex your arms energetically, breathing deeply, and open your eyes while silently uttering the cancellation formula: 'Arms firm, breathe deeply, open eyes.' Follow this with vigorous movements of your arms, legs, feet, fingers, toes, shoulders and neck, noting any areas of residual tension that remain in the arm. Repeat the entire exercise four times, allowing approximately one minute between each period to note the effects. Then focus your attention on your other arm and do the same as before.

Stage Two

Focus attention on each arm in turn, mentally rehearsing the suggestion 'My right/left arm is heavy and warm', using the same cancellation formula between each series as in Stage One. Do likewise for each leg.

Stage Three

Repeat the instruction 'Heartbeat calm and regular' four times for 90–180 seconds, with the cancellation instruction 'Breathe deeply, open eyes' and vigorous activity inserted between each period.

Stage Four
Focus on your breathing, repeating the phrase 'It breathes me' four times for 100–150 seconds, with a cancellation instruction between each series.

Stage Five
Repeat the instruction 'My solar plexus is warm' in the style of the previous stages, placing your hand over the area as you do so and imagining heat radiating from it.

Stage Six
Repeat the phrase 'My forehead is cool' in the style of the previous stages.

Schultz recommended that the entire series is practised three times daily, before meals and sleep. After a variable period of training it can be completed in a few minutes and the autogenic state of stability maintained for prolonged periods. When the standard series has been mastered, a series of exercises involving visualisation can be introduced. This 'meditative series' includes visualising certain colours which reinforce sensations of warmth or coolness, and progresses to visualisation of clouds, geometrical shapes, other persons, abstract concepts such as freedom, and selective states of feeling.

CREATIVE VISUALISATION AND GUIDED IMAGERY
Creative visualisation (discussed in Chapter Three) can be thought of as passive concentration on or witnessing of the contents of the mind by observing one's spontaneously produced images in a detached, unprejudiced manner, as though meditating or watching a silent movie. Guided imagery involves passive concentration on or witnessing of imaginative stimuli

provided by another person, as a spoken or written narrative. Both processes are in themselves highly relaxing because they absorb us fully, and when we are fully absorbed in this way, we not only gain awareness of and insight into aspects of ourselves of which we are ordinarily unaware, but may also gain control over these unconscious processes. The Indian sage Osho describes the process as 'getting into an attitude so deeply that the very attitude becomes reality'. He points to a technique called 'heat' yoga, practised by Tibetan lamas, where, by imagining themselves as a burning fire, they can withstand sub-zero temperatures even when naked. In a situation where their blood should freeze, their bodies become hot and they begin to perspire. As Osho observes, their bodies are really hot and the perspiration is real, but this reality is created solely through imagination because 'once you get in tune with your imagination, the body starts functioning. . . . Imagination is a force, an energy, and the mind moves through it. And when the mind moves through it, the body follows.'[9]

Certainly modern clinical research confirms that 'where the mind tends to focus, the emotions and physiology are likely to follow'.[10] Just as our worst imaginings can give rise to symptoms of stress and stress-related illness, so too visualisation procedures can decrease tension and effect positive physio-logical changes, enhance immune functioning and alter the course of any malignancy. As with the other methods examined above, visualisation can be used as a means of dealing with stress directly, and also indirectly by providing insight into how our belief systems and emotional responses contribute to stress. Visualisation exercises may not only help to promote awareness of feelings of hopelessness, helplessness, lack of control and lay bare the beliefs that undermine health and well-being, but may also enable us to gain a sense of control and bring about positive changes in attitude. Visualisation is not only an important motivational tool for attaining or recovering health; it is also an important means of achieving self-discovery and effecting positive change. As T. E. Lawrence once observed: 'The dreamers of the day are dangerous men, for they may act their dream with open eyes to make it possible.'[11]

Accordingly, visualisation is now widely and increasingly used in various applied fields. It is most effective if carried out daily for approximately twenty minutes, but it can be used intermittently to very good effect and combined with any other method of relaxation. Indeed it is a feature of all the approaches included here.

DREAMING

Creative visualisation and guided imagery can be thought of as waking dreams because they are in most respects similar to the dreams we have when asleep. The images produced have similar qualities: they are instantaneous and fleeting, convey a great deal of complex information simultaneously, and although vivid and powerful when experienced, they are quickly forgotten. Dreaming when asleep differs from waking dreams in as much as it occurs quite spontaneously and is not normally under our control. We all dream but inability to remember our dreams often leads us to think that we don't. In dreaming we experience the single-mindedness that may elude us otherwise, and we can gain insight into ourselves just as effectively in this state as when it is induced by the methods outlined above.

By attending to our dreams, we can often receive messages and valuable guidance normally obscured by the insistent chattering of our waking, rational mind. Indeed it is during dreaming that the non-verbal information stored and processed by our brain can be made available to us. Our dreams relay to us the information we glean through our everyday sensory experiences, interpersonal interactions, and so on. They are the medium by which are intuition, instincts, hunches, gut feelings and inspiration are communicated to us. When we dream of occurrences or events of the previous day, these aspects, which may have been overlooked, unheard, unrecognised or unidentified at the time, become more salient. Often the stressors of our lives of which we are ordinarily unconscious impress themselves on us in these dreams.

Certain dreams may embody particular stressors such as anxieties and fears and they may recur at times when these are of significance to us. They may be represented symbolically as certain objects, persons or situations. For example, at times of self-doubt and low self-confidence, Anna would dream that she was a high-school student studying for A-level examinations, as she had been many years previously. In this dream unaccountably she had missed most of the courses she was studying, lost all her course notes, or left herself insufficient time for revision. She experienced a dreadful sense of panic at the seemingly impossible task of learning the necessary material in the time available and an overwhelming fear of failure. The dream always concluded with her great relief at realising that she had successfully passed the examinations the previous year and had no need to re-sit them. Whenever she has this dream now, she takes it as a sign that at an unconscious level she fears failing in some area, that this fear and self-doubt is totally unjustified and needs to be addressed at a conscious level.

In this way dreams can help bring hidden or repressed issues such as these into the open where they can be dealt with. Sometimes they do so dramatically and forcefully and we regard them as nightmares. Nancy was terrorised by the same nightmare for years, to the extent that she feared sleep and would lie awake tense and anxious most nights. In the dream she was pursued down dark, sombre streets by a huge, menacing and unwavering eye. When eventually she sought help, she was encouraged to confront the eye by drawing the dream. In this way she came to recognise the eye as a symbol for herself, her 'I', which she was running away from rather than confronting a distressing experience that took place in her childhood. Most of her energy was bound up in this traumatic experience she had been unable to come to terms with, and which, as a result, remained painful, unfinished business for her. Not only did she have little energy available to her in the present because of this investment in her past, but what energy she did have was being exhausted through lack of sleep. As a result she was in poor health and unable to deal effectively with everyday life. When she acknowledged that her dream was demanding her to confront herself and resolve her unfinished business, she began to do so, the nightmare began to change, lose its menace and become much less frequent.

Dreams can also reveal the kinds of issues and concerns that drain our energy — particularly past experiences, relationships and unfinished business. They can be a rich source of clues as to the tensions and anxieties in our present life. Trying to remember your dreams and to learn the messages they convey about what is going on within you at deeper and ordinarily inaccessible levels is an important feature of achieving self-awareness and self-development. If you don't already do so, it is worth keeping a notebook by your bed and recording your dreams as soon as you awake. Quick jottings usually suffice to commit the dream to conscious verbal memory and you can scrutinise these later when you are fully awake. Dream records of this kind can be particularly helpful during periods of stress in your life, when the outer voices of your waking life may drown out your own intuition — literally your 'inner teaching' or wisdom — and its inner voice.

LISTENING TO YOUR INNER VOICE

The methods outlined above are all very effective in enabling us to distance ourselves from the insistent chattering in our heads and to create inner silence. They enable you to attain balance, to become the centre of the cyclone — the still space amidst the frenzied activity of life — and in the silence there to discover your own inner voice. By listening to this inner voice, as opposed to the many other voices of your life, you can begin to learn what you really think, feel, need and want rather than what others want you to think, feel and want. You can begin to find your real self as opposed to the self shaped to the requirements of others.

As a result you will find yourself no longer in two minds, torn between the demands of others and your own needs, and that the tensions generated by this inner conflict and dis-ease will disappear. You will realise that inner harmony is the key to healthy and creative living.

Nevertheless, it remains the case that relatively few people dedicate themselves to such a regular discipline, whether that of recording their dreams or spending as little as twenty minutes each day engaged in the other ways of becoming single-minded. Those least likely to make the time are those pressured, stressed individuals who would most benefit from doing so. Their excuse is typically that they can't find the time. This in itself denotes a passive rather than a proactive approach to managing their lives: time for ourselves isn't something we find but something we must make or take. The fact that such people do not indicates a lack of balance between their needs and other demands on them. It also suggests lack of self-control.

Mavis suffers from hypertension. She and her husband travelled a considerable distance every week to attend my evening class because Mavis relaxed during these sessions, and over the weeks her blood pressure reduced significantly, so much so that her consultant initially thought his readings were mistaken and repeated them. Despite this, Mavis insisted she could not relax except when at my class. It was not that she could not make the time to relax elsewhere — she and her husband spent two hours travelling to and from the class — but rather that Mavis believed that I 'made' her relax. She did not believe she had any control over herself. It was this belief that underpinned her hypertension because it was the major source of stress in her life.

Clearly reliance on others or the use of external aids to relaxation is counterproductive as all relaxation techniques are fundamentally a means of self-empowerment with the aim of encouraging self-control and self-reliance. For this reason it is preferable to avoid frequent use of pre-recorded relaxation tapes. These can be very useful in helping you to begin relaxation and to remember various relaxation techniques and exercises, but they can limit your experience to that dictated or defined by others. They can also become boring and tedious, and so produce rather than relieve tension. When you have mastered the basics of any relaxation technique, it is better to follow your own inclinations and modify procedures to suit yourself. It is especially important if you are incorporating visualisation in your relaxation to give full rein to your imagination. Remember that your spontaneously produced images provide the greatest insight into yourself and the important issues in your life, so do not feel that you have to follow the exercises in this book exactly. Regard them as guidelines rather than templates to be followed rigidly.

WEIGHING UP THE STRESSORS IN YOUR LIFE

A different way of achieving balance involves weighing up the various factors in your life and ridding yourself of those that produce unnecessary stress. Once again this is essentially a question of relaxing or letting go, as the following parable illustrates:

> Two monks who had forsworn all contact with women were walking from one monastery to another when they came upon a young woman stranded on the bank of a river swollen with floodwater. Seeing her distress, one of the monks carried the woman across the river before continuing his journey. His colleague berated him constantly for his sinful actions, insisting that he should not have touched the woman. When eventually they reached the monastery gates, he turned to his still-complaining companion and said, 'Look: I put that woman down on the river bank. You are still carrying her.'

Like the distressed monk, we often continue to subject ourselves to quite unnecessary stress, usually by persisting in outmoded habits that have long outlived their usefulness, or by continuing to relay old messages to ourselves that no longer have relevance to us or our lives.

Cathy exemplifies this problem that we all share to varying degrees. She is a single parent who admits to being stressed by time, or the lack of it, and suffers from hypertension for which she has received medication for many years. She is always on the go, trying to fit various activities, including two part-time jobs, around driving her secondary-school-aged son and daughter to and from their separate schools in a town some twelve miles from her home. She estimates that she spends at least two hours a day in her car and finds this particularly stressful. She is convinced that the stress in her life will be greatly reduced by moving to live in the same town as the children's schools, but over a two-year period the sale of her house has fallen through six times, for different reasons, adding further stress.

It hadn't occurred to Cathy, until it was pointed out to her, that there is no need to drive the children to school as there are school buses, and therefore no need to move house. Her two major stressors — the twice-daily school run and the sale of the house — can therefore be eliminated simply by arranging for the children to travel on the school bus.

So why hadn't Cathy seen this? Quite simply because she was locked into a habitual behaviour pattern established some years previously when the children were younger and there was no school bus, and a mind-tape message that tells her that such 'selfless' behaviour is expected from a good mother. The same mind tape tells her that as a single parent she should prove herself a good mother. She now sees that her children would probably prefer to travel on the school bus and that this would free a lot more time and energy for herself and reduce her level of stress.

Unlike Cathy, Sylvia was unaware that one of her major

activities was causing her stress. Indeed she regarded it as a pleasurable hobby. Sylvia bred and exhibited cats and spent a good deal of time, energy and money pursuing her hobby. For many years she eagerly looked forward to collecting her copy of the weekly newspaper that reported the activities of the cat fancy. Then she began to notice that as she read the paper she became physically very tense. This continued for some time but it was only when the tension became quite marked that she began to question her attitude to her hobby. She then realised that she had gained little or no enjoyment from it for some considerable time and that there were numerous aspects of it that she found stressful. Having realised this, she began to exhibit her cats less frequently and eventually stopped attending shows completely. She found that she enjoyed her cats much more as a result and no longer felt tense when reading her weekly paper.

You may wonder why Sylvia was for so long unaware of this source of stress in her life. Her explanation is simply that she had been attending shows for so long that it had never occurred to her not to, and she constantly told herself what others told her — that she *should* show her lovely cats. Indeed that is how she came to exhibit them in the first place — the breeder of her first cat had insisted she *should* do this, and everyone else's views concurred. Then, after a good deal of success, it seemed to her, and others, that she *should* continue. As she said:

> 'Even when I realised I was no longer happy showing the cats, I kept telling myself that after all the time and money I've put into this pastime I shouldn't give up.'

Like Cathy and Sylvia, you may be able to identify features in your life that are causing you quite unnecessary and unavoidable stress, and, having identified them, you can quite easily let go of them. The following visualisation exercise may help you to pinpoint them.

EXERCISE SEVEN

HANDLING YOUR BAGGAGE

Imagine that you are on a journey and that you are carrying some baggage. Notice where you are travelling and how and what you are carrying. Be aware of the weight of your baggage. Does it seem too heavy, rather light or just about right? If you are unsure, imagine carrying the baggage some distance and observing how it feels. If the baggage feels heavy, begin to unpack the contents and to observe these closely. Notice the various items and your reactions to them. Are there any items that surprise you in any way? If so, how? Do any of the items belong to other people? If so, what are these items and to whom do they belong? Why are you carrying them? How are the items packed, and in what order? Make sure you examine all the items, especially those at the very bottom of the baggage.

When you have done this, decide which of the items you can do without and repack the baggage. Imagine picking it up. If it feels lighter and more comfortable, decide how you are going to dispose of the rejected items. If, on picking up the baggage, it still feels heavy or uncomfortable, reorganise the contents, discarding enough items to make it light and easy to carry. Be aware of your feelings about sorting through and discarding various items, especially those items which seem particularly difficult to dispose of. When you feel that you are able to travel light, continue your journey noticing any differences you may feel. Then allow the imagery to fade and return to ordinary awareness.

REACTIONS TO THE EXERCISE

Dispensing with Unnecessary Baggage

Most of us carry baggage in our journey through life in the form of messages, directives, instructions, rules, codes of conduct, expectations, attitudes, beliefs, ideals, standards, hopes, dreams and ambitions that we have acquired from others. These form the mind tapes or mental records that provide a continuous and seemingly unavoidable commentary on our activities. In some cases this baggage can weigh very heavily indeed and cause a good deal of stress and strain; sometimes this baggage feels painful. It is perhaps true to say that few of us travel light. Nevertheless, we may be so accustomed to this burden that we are unaware we are carrying it, much less its contents or source. We are therefore unaware that much of it is avoidable. Frequently our responses to the above exercise surprise us. They can also provide us with great relief.

Darryl imagined himself walking in open moorland on a blustery day and carrying a heavy rucksack on his back. He was surprised when he unpacked the imaginary rucksack to find a set of large spanners underneath the other contents. He certainly hadn't packed them as he could see no need for them. He then realised that these were his father's spanners. His father had been a working-class man from the north-east of England who held him, the eldest son, in absolute contempt for having pursued an academic calling rather than a suitably manly career in a shipyard or engineering firm. Throughout his life Darryl, now in his thirties, had been criticised and ostracised within the family for his interest in books, art and literature. He was quite clear what he *should* have been and that, having failed his father in such a fundamental way, he constantly tried to prove his worth to him, and was still doing so although his father had long since died. Darryl attributed his recurrent bouts of severe depression to his experiences in the family and saw the spanners as an indication that he still carried his father's values, attitudes and judgments with him. These were a constant, albeit largely unconscious, source of stress and tension and he realised that they underpinned his problems and had to be addressed in order for him to move on or progress satisfactorily in his life. By letting go of these stressors and 'downing tools', he could relieve himself of an enormous burden and take a great weight off his shoulders.

Kath imagined herself walking on a clifftop carrying a rucksack containing various items, some of which she realised she didn't need and later discarded simply by throwing them over the cliff. The items included her bathrobe, which although bulky, provides her with a great deal of comfort and enables her to relax, and sweaters belonging to other people, some in shades and sizes she wouldn't or couldn't wear. She was able to recognise these as symbols for various 'colourful' and impractical ideas she had picked up from others throughout her life. However, she was most surprised to notice that all these items were packed into a dirty old rucksack owned by her ex-husband. After a good deal of self-analysis, she recognised that she was still living her life according to his dictates and demands and that this was the major source of stress for her. She realised she no longer needed to do so. Nevertheless, she was reluctant to discard the rucksack as she had no other means of carrying her baggage. She interpreted this as an indication that she was not independent from her former husband, not self-sufficient and urgently in need of a new frame of reference for herself and her life. Following this insight, she imagined throwing away the rucksack and packing her undiscarded belongings into a milk pail which was easy to handle and carry and much more useful.

Reassessing the Essentials

Helen's first impression of her baggage — a rucksack — was that it was too light. She laid out all its contents — a camera, cagoule, Swiss army knife, aluminium saucepan and cutlery, plastic cup, plate and bowl, washbag, medical kit, sewing kit, towel, shorts, shirt, sweater, pair of trainers, torch, notepad and pens — and realised she hadn't packed her tent, sleeping bag and camping gas stove. She began to worry that if she did pack these, she wouldn't be able to carry the rucksack very far. Immediately she began to think that it would be easier if she had someone else to share the load, or used a bicycle. She then realised that these would actually add to her burden and restrict her freedom of movement. Helen wanted to travel as light as possible but also realised that she needed to be independent and self-sufficient, and that a tent was essential, not only for this reason but also because she needed privacy. In this way she acknowledged not only her essential needs but also that for her the main stressor in life is the tension between independence and freedom on the one hand, and too many responsibilities and ties on the other.

Like Helen, you may find that your baggage is initially light because it lacks important items that you need. In this way you may gain a better understanding of the needs you neglect and the features of your life that require reorganisation in order to accommodate them better.

Different Types of Baggage

Other aspects of this exercise may yield insight into the stressors of your life and the way you deal with them. Rucksacks and backpacks may reveal a tendency to put your problems out of sight rather than be 'up front' about them and that you tend to carry a weight on your shoulders. If this is so, you probably feel tension predominantly in your neck, back and shoulders, whereas if you imagine hand luggage you may experience more tension in your arms, especially the forearms.

The kind of baggage you imagine may also provide insights into some of the life issues that are significant for you. Andrew imagined carrying a doctor's bag which he associated with the professionalism and status he is striving towards. Carrie also imagined a doctor's bag but associated it with caring for others — something she feels is expected of her. Liz imagined a tapestry carpet bag, which while soft and feminine in appearance also had connotations of domesticity, carpets being something that need cleaning and shampooing and also can be walked all over. She realised that her baggage reflects both the positive and negative aspects of the female stereotype she struggles with in her life. Sarah was surprised to find a pair of pink panties on the top of her load. They weren't hers but she realised that they represented the ideals of femininity she had been encouraged to believe she should live up to. Amy imagined a Marks and Spencer's carrier bag which was light and easy to carry but which on closer examination revealed the middle-class, middle-of-the-road values and aspirations of her family, and the major source of conflict and stress in her life. Rosemary was carrying golf clubs belonging to a former boyfriend for her current partner, which made her realise she was transferring emotional baggage from one relationship to the other. Denise could clearly see an expensive Gucci bag, but when it came to looking inside it, she imagined going into a strange kitchen and making herself a cup of coffee. She realised that by doing so she was avoiding looking at her problems and that coffee drinking is one of the ways she copes with her anxiety.

You may have found that the above exercise helped you to identify the unnecessary stressors in your life. By eliminating as many as of these as you can, you will find that you free energy that you can use more positively and effectively. Furthermore, by sorting your priorities in this way, you may be able to achieve and maintain greater balance in your life. As a result you are likely to feel more in tune with yourself; more at ease, less tense, anxious and uncomfortable, and more in control of yourself and your life — to feel you are pulling your own strings rather than having them pulled for you.

KEY POINTS

1. Although avoiding stress altogether is widely advocated, it is neither feasible nor sensible. Your brain strives to achieve a balance that you need between under- and overstimulation. The difficulty in achieving the level of stimulation appropriate to your needs is that it is usually obscured by the demands others make on you.

2. To achieve balance you need to identify the demands of your lifescripts which are relayed to you by way of constant mental chatter. This requires you to become more single-minded.

3. You can become more single-minded via meditation, hypnosis, the Relaxation Response, Autogenic Training, creative visualisation and guided imagery, and analysing your dreams.

4. These methods bring about mental harmony, which produces beneficial psychological effects including reduced anxiety, improved mood, a more positive attitude, increased self-control, and a hypometabolic state physiologically characterised by quiescence, which is opposite to the state of high arousal induced by stress.

5. These approaches are also effective in creating inner silence and helping you to listen to your own inner voice and its needs, as opposed to the other voices in your life.

6. By listening to your inner voice, you can begin to learn what you really think, feel, need and want, and who you really are.

7. You can also achieve balance by weighing up and eliminating the unnecessary stressors of your life. Exercises in visualisation can help you to do so.

BEFRIENDING
YOURSELF

We have to change our patterns of reacting to experience.
For our problems do not lie in what we experience, but in
the attitude we have towards it.

Akong Rimpoche

OWNING YOUR BEHAVIOUR

Exercise Seven in the previous chapter may have helped you to
identify which aspects of your life you can't get on with and can
do without. You may find that you can drop some of them quite
easily, and that by eliminating these unnecessary stressors you
can release energy. However, you are very fortunate indeed if
you can deal with all your stressors in this way. Almost certainly
there will be some aspect of your life that isn't so easily
managed, and it may be a major feature such as an important
relationship, your job, financial matters or your health. You
may not like where you live, or who you are living with, your
job, the way you look or the way you feel. You may live alone
or be in poor health. Some of these circumstances you may be
able to change. Some you won't be able to change, but you can
change your attitude to them.

Ultimately it is not these circumstances that are the source of
your stress, but rather the way you view or interpret them. You

may feel that you loathe where you live, hate your job, detest your boss, can't get on with housework and are ill-disposed to your neighbours, and as with anyone or thing you regard as a foe or enemy you will feel uneasy, uncomfortable, anxious, tense, threatened and believe that 'they' make you feel this way. *They* don't; *you* do. You allow yourself to be angered or upset by them. Those people and events don't have to produce these responses; the anger or upset is yours. It was you who brought it into the situation, not the event or the other person. To suppose otherwise and think that your behaviour is dependent upon another person or a situation is to disown your own behaviour and your responsibility for it, and to give control of that behaviour away to the person or event. Nevertheless you can take control simply by changing how you respond. It is your decision whether to become angry, upset or not. A Chinese proverb expresses this very well: 'That the birds of worry and care fly above your head, this you cannot change, but that they build nests in your hair, this you can prevent.'

PERSONAL RESPONSIBILITY AND CHOICE

Applying this concept to stress, it is *your* decision whether or not to increase your blood pressure, heart and pulse rates, to become tense and anxious; and it is also *your* decision whether or not you will regularly practise relaxation techniques. Practising these is a good example of taking control and assuming responsibility for, or owning, your behaviour. Many of the people who express interest in practising relaxation do not actually do so, and many of those who begin often do not continue. The excuse most commonly given by such people is that they haven't time. They do have time, but they choose to use it for other purposes. Some choose to believe that they cannot relax without the guidance of others. Others claim that there is nowhere they can relax, or insufficient quiet for them to be able to do so. These are their choices; they are responsible for them and must accept the consequences. If you choose to relax, you can do so any time, any place and anywhere.

Once you realise that you have this choice, you can act on it, or not. It is your choice, as intrepid traveller Christina Dodwell indicates: 'I was alone, lost in wild mountains at night, and I was still scared of the dark. I had two options: either I could huddle in my cave and sink into terror, or I could disregard my nervousness and sleep soundly in my cosy grass bed. . . . I slept a deep untroubled sleep.'[1]

In any situation there are good and bad, positive and negative elements. Like Christina Dodwell, we all have a choice as to whether we focus on the positive or the negative aspects of our circumstances, and as her comment shows, this choice determines our experience of that situation.

Dave and Elaine met Robin and Yvonne when they were travelling in the Middle East. They quickly realised that Robin became easily stressed. If everything didn't run like clockwork, he became agitated and anxious, and as little runs like clockwork in the Middle East this meant he was upset much of the time. Whereas the others thoroughly enjoyed the time spent at borders, immigration points, ferry terminals and the like because they provided opportunities to observe the local colour and customs and to meet the people, Robin regarded it as time wasted and he would wander about fretfully, frequently looking at his watch and growing more and more impatient and irritable. Before long he began to irritate Dave and Elaine, who noticed that he also taxed Yvonne's patience. When they were travelling through the most spectacular landscapes or visiting wonderful sights, standing silently in awed reverence or wonder, Robin would begin to talk about cars, cameras or sights he'd seen elsewhere in the world. He could not be quiet or still, and was never centred in the here and now because his attention was always somewhere else. Dave and Elaine decided that they had a choice: they could continue to let Robin annoy them and ruin their journey, or they could ignore his foibles. Opting for the latter, they began to find his behaviour amusing, but also to feel sorry for him as they realised that life passed Robin by completely and that, although he had travelled widely and seen a good deal, he had perceived little.

On the evening before the two couples went their separate ways, they stopped at a hotel for a meal. It was out of season and so, despite a sizeable and impressive menu, their choices were limited to only three dishes, one for each course. This was not a problem until Robin discovered that the dessert on offer was not to his liking. This upset him greatly, and for the remainder of the evening he could talk of nothing else. He was still complaining about it the following day and when later that day the couples said their farewells, it was clear that this one event had become the major issue for Robin and had ruined not simply his evening but the entire trip.

Robin is typical of those people who habitually experience stress. Not only does he focus on the negative and worst aspects of events and situations, but he also cannot let go of them, brooding on them and inflating them out of all proportion. In contrast, Dave, Elaine and Yvonne, with their more positive attitude, saw little to stress them and were able to let go of minor irritations and disappointments rather than allow them to plague them and disrupt their enjoyment. They were able to remain calm and relaxed while Robin made himself tense and anxious. These reactions are a matter of choice, not destiny. As Hamlet observes: 'There is nothing either good or bad, but thinking makes it so.'[2] We choose whether or not to raise our blood pressure, level of cholesterol, heart rate and muscle tension — although we may not realise this — by adopting a certain attitude or way of thinking.

MAKING BAD CHOICES

We are all free to choose what we think, although most of us don't exercise this control over our thoughts but allow them to be dictated to by others. To complicate matters further, we have been taught to be critical rather than positive, to focus on the bad rather than the good. This is evident when we are complimented. Told how well we look or that our work is good, we tend to deny or trivialise the observation. We may say, 'No; really, I look awful,' or 'It was nothing.' How many of us have heard the cook present us with a meal saying, 'I don't think this will be up to much'?

Many people are so focused on the negative that they perceive everything in this way. They interpret any comment as criticism, and tend to think that everyone is always 'getting at' or attacking them. Moreover, this negativity isn't confined to their dealings with others; situations also conspire against them. These are the people who typically say, 'It always happens to me,' and think that they have bad luck, rather than bad judgment. Unsurprisingly, such people often try to cope by avoiding certain situations or distracting themselves with alcohol, drugs, food, television, social interactions and sexual promiscuity. This kind of 'avoidance coping' can be useful when the problem is insoluble, but when something can be done to alter it but is not, it remains a stressor and is more likely to produce chronic stress and consequent illness.

REAPPRAISING THE SITUATION

Confronted with similar stressors, others may appraise them in such a way as to avoid stress. They are able to act in the face of a stressor in a way that minimises or eliminates its threat. This idea is conveyed by the Chinese word for *crisis*, which is composed of two characters that separately mean 'danger' and 'opportunity'. Implicitly, therefore, every crisis presents these two features, and our response depends on which view of it we favour.

Psychologist Suzanne Kobasa and her colleagues have found that differences in the appraisal of a situation can result in enormous differences in how people respond to potentially stressful events and in the amount of stress they experience. In a study conducted at the Bell Telephone Company, Illinois, during a prolonged and uncertain period of wide-sweeping and major reorganisation, they found that half the executives experienced high levels of illness whereas the other half remained healthy. The latter were similar in terms of income, job status, educational levels, age, ethnic background and religious affiliation but their attitudes towards themselves, their jobs and fellow workers were totally different. Characteristically these executives had a strong commitment to themselves, their work and families; a sense of control over their lives; and an ability to see change in their life as a challenge rather than a threat. They accepted that change, rather than stability, is the norm in life and welcomed it as an opportunity for growth and self-development. They sought novelty, tolerated ambiguity and showed mental flexibility and a strong sense of purpose in dealing with life's problems. Moreover, they looked to other people for support when they needed it.

By comparison, the executives who were less hardy experienced a sense of powerlessness, were threatened by change, anxious in the face of uncertainty and lacked social support. However, their most marked characteristic was alienation, not only from themselves but also from others. In other words, these non-hardy types experienced their world and others as unfriendly and hostile.

Subsequently the characteristics of psychological hardiness identified in this study — commitment, control and challenge — were confirmed in studies of managers, other professional groups and women visiting gynaecologists. However, an interesting factor emerged in a study of US army officers. While a sense of commitment and control appeared to protect officers against stress, those who were oriented towards challenge were in fact *more* prone to illness. When a person's need for stimulation is not matched by the opportunities for it, *more* illness can result, and in the post-Vietnam army there was little room for those seeking novelty or challenge. The results of the army study therefore highlight the importance of finding the proper balance of stimulation and challenge in life.

In an attempt to engender a sense of commitment, control and challenge, psychologist Suzanne Kobasa, along with the psychiatrist Salvatore Maadi, developed 'hardiness induction groups' in which highly stressed, hypertensive executives were helped to cope with stressors by appraising themselves and their stressors positively. After eight weekly sessions, the executives scored higher on tests of hardiness, reported fewer symptoms of psychological stress and their blood pressure was found to be lower when compared with executives in an untreated control group. This study shows that people can learn to avoid the negative consequences of stress, simply by 'befriending' it.[3]

BEFRIENDING STRESS

How do we make friends with stress? We do so in the same way that we make friends with anyone or anything. We don't make friends with others by avoiding them or by viewing them negatively. We tend to regard friends positively and also to feel positively towards them. They are usually people we accept easily and with whom we can relax, feel comfortable, express ourselves and have a laugh.

However, as we've seen, it is *we* who inflict much of the stress we suffer on ourselves through the way we perceive, appraise, think about and respond to events and situations. In as much as we are the source of this stress, we are our own worst enemies. Accordingly it is ourselves we need to befriend.

ACCEPTING YOURSELF

Underpinning much of the stress we subject ourselves to is our belief that we should conform to the demands of others and shape ourselves accordingly. Simply accepting ourselves for what we are rather than what we think we should be relieves the stress created by this pressure to conform. Resistance to being ourselves causes tension. When we accept any situation, we stop resisting it and relax the tensions involved. As a result the situation changes. Likewise, when you accept yourself as you are, then you change. Instead of being your own worst enemy, you become your own best friend.

Instead of making demands on yourself to be as you imagine others want you to be, you allow yourself to be who and what you are, and accept yourself as this. Moreover, you regard yourself, as you would a friend, positively; as having value and worth.

You can gain some insight into how you currently appraise yourself by sitting silently and noticing or witnessing (see Chapter Four) the chatter in your mind. Try the following exercise.

EXERCISE EIGHT

WITNESSING IN SILENCE

Find somewhere you can sit or lie comfortably. Having done this, gradually withdraw your attention from your surroundings and focus attention on yourself. Simply be aware of the thoughts and feelings that arise as you do so. Observe them as you might watch a flock of sheep, or clouds in the sky. Notice how they come and go; what they do; how they interact; and do so objectively without making any judgment. Continue to observe yourself in this way for 15–20 minutes.

REACTIONS TO THE EXERCISE

After 'witnessing' herself for only one session, Ellen, a complementary therapist by profession, realised that she constantly put herself down by giving herself negative messages. She found herself observing her behaviour throughout the day and was shocked to discover how often and how well she relays the same messages to others. When someone responded to this by asking if she'd left her self-esteem at home, she heard herself reply, 'No. I've got none.' She also realised that she often provides others with ammunition to fire back at her. For example, a new client told her that she had found it difficult to make initial contact because Ellen had no telephone. Instead of explaining why she was temporarily without a phone, Ellen said, 'It's not very professional is it?', to which the prospective client replied, 'You're right; it's not very professional,' and walked out.

Later the same day, Ellen declined payment for a talk she had been invited to give to a women's group, and only afterwards realised that her difficulties in accepting money result largely from her poor view of her own worth. After a week of witnessing and observing herself in this way, a horrified Ellen concluded that she compulsively portrayed herself in the worst possible light and by so doing gave power away to others. She realised she had to learn to give herself and others different, more positive messages, and she had to start by thinking positively.

THINKING POSITIVELY ABOUT YOURSELF

This isn't simply saying nice things to yourself or 'geeing yourself up', as is often supposed. It involves relaxing and imagining very vivid scenes that you associate with specific, positive emotions such as joy and tranquillity. In this way you can create a state of private peacefulness that often will counteract the anxiety aroused by the more negative thoughts and imaginings you typically relay to yourself. Positive thinking involves learning how to distract yourself from recurring painful or frightening thoughts by developing a repertoire of positive images to draw on during periods of stress. Once you can absorb your mind in this way, the 'volume control' of your usual mental chatter is turned down. Not only does this quieten the negative messages normally relayed by the conscious mind, but it makes the unconscious part of your mind more open to suggestion, which can be highly effective in bringing about both psychological and physical change.

Auto-Suggestion

The effectiveness of self-administered suggestion was amply demonstrated by Émile Coué, who treated some 40,000 people in this way before the First World War and claimed a 97 per cent success rate in overcoming his clients' problems. Coué's method, which he termed *auto-suggestion*, was to relax clients so they were amenable to assistance and then give them a series of positive suggestions or affirmations intended to promote psychological and physical well-being. These affirmations were repeated by the clients periodically until there was a marked improvement in their condition. Coué also insisted that his clients repeat 15–20 times daily, while in bed, the phrase 'Every day in every way, I'm getting better and better', which is often associated with Mary Baker Eddy, the founder of Christian Science, who was greatly influenced by Coué.

The simplicity of auto-suggestion led to its falling into disrepute because practitioners urged their clients simply to repeat relevant suggestions, and ignored Coué's preparatory work in relaxing the person. However, it has since been demonstrated that, using auto-suggestion, the heart can be speeded up or slowed down,[4] near-sighted people can change the shape of their eyeballs and improve long-distance vision, and stomach contractions resulting from hunger can be eliminated.[5] Indeed most of the effects of hypnosis and Autogenic Training are achieved in this way.

A study at St Thomas's Hospital, London, has shown that women receiving positive affirmations via headphones prior to surgery for hysterectomy recover much more quickly after the operation than do control groups — their temperature is lower, they feel less pain, can relax more and be discharged from hospital much sooner.[6] Recognition of the power of auto-suggestion has led many therapists to encourage positive thinking in their clients, and positive affirmations are an important feature of self-help approaches.

To be effective, positive affirmations should be short,

positive, tailored to the individual and delivered in the present tense. They should also be unambiguous and specific and, as far as is possible, embody the desired outcome. So, instead of saying, 'Cinderella will go to the ball,' an affirmation should state, 'I am having a ball right now.' This is not lying or self-deception but rather a means of self-direction; what is being suggested here is the desired outcome rather than what is actually happening at the time. You may prefer suggestions such as: 'I am now bringing more and more [of whatever it is you need — love, peace, harmony, support, joy, fulfilment] into my life.'

EXPRESSING YOURSELF

As we have seen in Chapters One and Two, *suppressing* rather than *expressing* yourself is a major source of stress that arises from doing as we are told and what we think we *should* do rather than what we *want* to do. With friends we can often express ourselves more openly than with less intimate acquaintances and this is in itself therapeutic. We may unburden ourselves of problems by getting off our chest some of the pent-up frustration, anger, irritation or sadness we feel, or by engaging in activities with them that enable us to do so in other ways. A game of squash may be a very effective way of thrashing out our problems, and a chat about our problems during a round of golf or a cross-country hike may provide a new perspective on them. Not surprisingly, therefore, social support emerges as an important buffer between ourselves and stress and stress-related illness, and those who have and take advantage of it fare better than those who don't.

Being able to be open and caring with others is one of the key ways of developing social-support networks. However, we are not always able to express our feelings even to our closest friends. This is usually because we have internalised very powerful messages throughout life that tell us that we *should* control the expression of certain emotions, and we fear the consequences of doing otherwise. Females typically learn to control the expression of anger, aggression and sexuality, whereas males learn not to express vulnerability, sentimentality and affection. It is often easier and less threatening to stay aloof and detached from others. Fear prevents us getting close to them; fear that if we show love, we will be rejected, ridiculed and embarrassed, that we will find ourselves unable to be intimate, caring and loving.

To develop social-support systems we have to overcome these fears and express ourselves. If we don't take advantage of the opportunities that are presented to us, we may never another have another chance. By doing so, we improve our social-support network, and the love, involvement and care we give to others is given back to us, helping us to be more effective in managing the stress of our lives.

The converse is also true: those of us who don't express our feelings to those we care about often live to regret it and this can become a major source of stress in our lives. Many people admit that they would feel so much better now 'if only' they had told their parents, partners, children, friends or colleagues that they loved or valued them before they lost them through death, divorce, disability or living apart.

LETTING GO OF THE PAST

Keeping the past alive requires energy. You are using your life force to keep old memories alive rather than focusing it on the present. Taking back energy from the past effectively shifts your epicentre of power, maximising the energy available to you here and now.

Agonising over what we should have done in various situations is in itself a source of stress. By holding on to the past in this way we generate tension which manifests itself both mentally and physically. A good deal of our energy can therefore be locked up in our past and is not available to us on a daily basis. It is important to let go of the past so that we can view it impersonally, or dispassionately. This is not a denial of the past; simply distancing yourself from it so that it no longer affects you emotionally.

For many years Janice felt great resentment towards her mother-in-law for the dismissive way she had always treated her. This had created difficulties in her relationship with her husband and contributed significantly to Janice's nervous breakdown quite early in their marriage. Over the years Janice's relationship with her mother-in-law ostensibly improved but anger and dislike remained just below the surface and would erupt, sometimes quite violently and usually very destructively, in her dealings with her husband. It took Janice a long, long time to realise that her mother-in-law's behaviour was not directed towards her personally, but would have been directed to anyone who had 'taken' her son from her. Once she recognised this, Janice was able to regard the situation impersonally and no longer allow it to affect her emotionally.

LETTING GO OF YOUR ANGER

Expressing negative emotions is also important. If we don't express these feelings, they tend to build up within us and cause tension and greater stress, as is conveyed in William Blake's poem 'A Poison Tree':

> *I was angry with my friend,*
> *I told my wrath, my wrath did end.*
> *I was angry with my foe:*
> *I told it not, my wrath did grow.*

However, we can express our feelings, positive or negative, in many ways other than through speech. We can express them through such activities as writing, painting, sculpting, singing, dancing, playing musical instruments, acting, gardening, cooking, swimming, keeping fit, and an endless variety of sporting and leisure pursuits — if we only choose to.

INDULGING YOURSELF

Many of us choose to do otherwise, though. We may tell ourselves that we cannot do these things. We are even more likely to tell ourselves that we can't do them because we *should* be doing something else — usually something others want us to do or that we think they expect from us. As we have seen in Chapter One, people who don't satisfy their needs are likely to be stressed and to become ill as a result. Expressing themselves, much less acting so as to satisfy their needs, is often very difficult for them. Even admitting their needs to themselves may be difficult because they have learned to consider it selfish and that they *should* be selfless. To acknowledge one's needs is therefore an admission of failure. While it is good to want to live for others, it is nevertheless important to recognise that we can only be selfless once we have a 'self'. Without a proper sense of self, we have nothing of value to give to others.

In working with countless people over many years, I have found denial of personal needs to be the major trigger for stress, and psychological and physical illness. It is always rooted in lack of self-esteem — or self-worth. Basically, people who don't think they amount to much don't see their needs as 'worth' bothering about. They don't think they deserve time for themselves, don't care for themselves and don't expect others to; and illness thrives in this culture of self-neglect. To reverse the situation you have to learn self-respect. I therefore set 'homework' for those people I work with individually and warn them in advance that they will find it difficult, and perhaps even impossible initially. However, my guidelines help them to give permission to themselves to be self-indulgent — for once — and to date no one has failed to do so. You might like to set yourself some homework of your own with this simple exercise.

EXERCISE NINE

TREATING YOURSELF WELL

When you wake up each morning, take some time to decide on just one thing that you really want to do during the day, or want not to do, and act on this decision. Begin by deciding on something quite simple, such as taking a leisurely bath rather than a short shower, or not washing up after dinner as usual. Keep a daily record of the decision-making process and the conflicts and difficulties you anticipate resulting from this decision, and your feelings and responses having acted on it. Continue to do this every morning for a week. Having done so, decide on two things you really want to do or not each day for a further week, and keep a record as before. Then the following week decide on three things you want to do or not, act on these decisions and record your responses.

REACTIONS TO THE EXERCISE

I set Marjory this exercise. She was very stressed because of her increasingly frequent outbursts of 'irrational' anger and tears directed at Bill, her companion of many years since the death of her husband, and a confirmed bachelor. Bill frequently failed to turn up for evening meals Marjory had prepared, excluded her from social engagements with his friends and let her down over joint arrangements such as outings and holidays, and even birthday treats. Marjory was often hurt by his thoughtlessness, but nevertheless considered herself at fault because she had been taught that she *should* never express anger and *should not* be selfish. As a wife and mother, she had always put the needs of her husband and family before her own and she had no recollection of ever expressing her needs to anyone. She wasn't even sure she had any. As a result, she regarded the exercise as a real challenge.

The first day Marjory decided that she would like fish for her evening meal. Bill didn't like fish so she never bought it. She went to the supermarket to buy the fish and also filled her basket with all the other foods she likes but never buys in deference to Bill's preferences. She felt a sense of elation and powerfulness she hadn't experienced previously. That evening she cooked herself the fish and something else for Bill. The following day she told Bill that she would like to watch a wildlife programme on television instead of football, which she endured only because he liked it. On the third day she decided against her weekly visit to a friend after which she usually feels depressed. In these simple ways Marjory began to assert herself and, at the age of eighty, became a new woman. She found that not only did she feel much less stressed but also that Bill appreciated not having to take responsibility for every decision and was more considerate of her needs.

Like Marjory, Jean realised she spent most of her time meeting other people's needs rather than her own and this was her major source of stress. She decided to say 'no' to her friend when she asked if she could pop in for a quick chat, which from past experience Jean knew would involve several hours of listening to her problems, and had the early night she had promised herself.

As Marjory and Jean discovered, indulging yourself in these small ways is fulfilling in the very real sense that you are filling your life with what you want rather than what others want of you. Indulging yourself in these ways is also empowering because expressing yourself and satisfying your own needs, while not hurting others in the process, is being assertive.

ASSERTING YOURSELF

Learning to say 'no' without experiencing guilt about doing so is the key to asserting yourself and is for most people a major step in the direction of stress relief. This is because by acting assertively you are usually fulfilling your needs while maintaining effective interpersonal relationships. Whereas if you generally act non-assertively, you are not satisfying your needs, and those unsatisfied needs will become stressors. You are probably also becoming a stressor for others.

Wendy, for example, never makes a decision. When asked by family and friends what she would like, or wants to do, she always replies, 'I don't mind. I'll do/have whatever you want.' Not only does this place responsibility on others but its also means she can blame them when things are not to her liking. She then takes offence at their impatience and annoyance when she tells them that they should know that she's never liked whatever they have chosen on her behalf. She sees them as aggressive when in fact she is the aggressor.

Many people confuse assertiveness with aggressiveness. The difference between these is that aggression is a hostile or destructive pattern of thinking or behaviour that is harmful to others, whereas assertiveness is putting yourself forward or standing up for yourself in a way that is positive and non-harmful to them. If you generally behave aggressively, your needs are met but at the expense of others, and the poor interpersonal relationships you create become stressors for yourself and others.

TAKING YOUR TIME

Asserting yourself is also a fundamental requirement of time management, which most stressed individuals typically don't achieve very satisfactorily. Usually this is because they spend their time meeting other people's demands and as a result have no time to become aware of their needs, much less fulfil them. Underpinning most people's difficulty in saying 'no' are the beliefs that they *should* acquiesce to others and that they will be punished in some way for not doing so. As a result they find themselves with 'punishing' schedules instead and stress that is damaging to their health and well-being rather than enhancing their self-image.

Broadly, people experience time in one of two ways: as being on their side, or against them — that is, as friend or foe. Those who are friendly with time are typically more leisurely and unhurried in their approach to life, and work at their own pace. They are generally well organised and efficient, and set realistic goals and deadlines. As a result they tend to meet schedules and keep appointments. They are able to make time for other people, whether family, friends or work colleagues, to take time for their interests, leisure activities and holidays, and to enjoy themselves.

The lifestyle of those in conflict with time is very different. They possess a sense of urgency, usually attempt to do too much too quickly and expect immediate results. Their objectives and schedules are unrealistic, and consequently they never have enough time. They are constantly rushing to meet deadlines and keep appointments, and are often late for both; or they make excessive demands on themselves, working day and night to achieve their aims. They tend to hurry and panic, to leave tasks unfinished, to give insufficient attention to them, or to put them off until later. As a result they tend to create a backlog of uncompleted tasks, and so either cannot make time for leisure activities and holidays, or feel guilty if they do. They are constantly under pressure and stressed.

Although often inefficient themselves, they tend to be impatient with others, whom they expect to respond immediately to their requests or demands. Such people typically take little time to consider the needs of others. Not surprisingly they tend to create pressures for, and tensions in, those around them. For such people time is not simply a foe but a potentially deadly enemy.

Extensive clinical research conducted since the 1970s has established that individuals who are constantly 'up against time' typically have high blood pressure, elevated levels of blood hormones, and increased respiratory rate, sweat-gland activity and muscle tension. Not only do they show signs of stress but some 28 per cent of them exhibit clear signs of coronary heart disease, compared with only 4 per cent of 'time-friendly' persons. They are also significantly more likely to succumb to hypertension, migraine, gastro-intestinal problems, stroke, kidney disease and other stress-related disorders, which have collectively been described as 'time' or 'hurry' sickness. Indeed such people are more susceptible to virtually every kind of illness and are significantly more likely to die suddenly and at a relatively early age.[7] Fortunately it is possible to modify this personality style, which is referred to as 'Type A' personality. This is not simply a matter of trying to slow down but of becoming aware of your real needs and giving yourself permission to act on them.

AMUSING YOURSELF
HUMOUR

While humour is recognised as a vital ingredient in the formation and maintenance of friendships, its importance in dealing with stress is often overlooked. Yet a sense of humour enables us to see the funny side of situations that might otherwise be stressful, and also to take ourselves less seriously. Sigmund Freud observed that humour is liberating because it enables us not to be distressed by the provocations of life, and not be compelled to suffer its traumas.[8] An essential element of humour is that it shows us that life's traumas can also be opportunities for pleasure. Humour is a state of mind in which we reassert our invulnerability and refuse to submit to threat and fear. It puts a new perspective on our stressors and alters our attitude and response to them. Hence James Thurber's statement: 'Humour is the only solvent of terror and tension.'[9]

Humour is healthy not only because it can relieve stress in these ways, and is pleasurable, but also because it is 'wholesome' — it helps us become *whole*. The Buddha, who saw the cosmic 'joke' or truth of the whole universe, rather than the illusory and fragmented universe our rational mind tricks us into perceiving, personifies the Eastern belief in the wholesome nature of humour. As the Indian sage Osho has observed, it 'joins our split parts' and 'glues our fragments into one whole'.[10] It is therefore the very antithesis of breakdown. The teacher of Tibetan wisdom Ngakpa Chogyam indicates: 'When we discover that we create our own sense of unfulfilment, and maintain it only through constant effort, we may well burst out laughing!'[11]

LAUGHTER

Laughter is an observable reaction to humour. Sir Max Beerbohm once observed: 'Strange, when you come to think of it, that of all the countless folk who have lived before our time on this planet not one is known in history or legend as having died of laughter.'[12] Laughter is life-giving; it is the best medicine. There is nothing new in such a view; indeed, some four hundred years ago mirth was considered sufficient cure in itself. Psychologically laughter is inconsistent with anger, which can precipitate heart attacks, and with depression, which is widely considered a factor in the onset of many cancers and in many other diseases associated with suppression of the immune system.

Claims regarding the beneficial effects of laughter focus on neuro-transmitters — chemicals secreted by the brain, immune system and certain nerve cells — that send messages from one to the other. The preliminary results of studies lend support to the theory that laughter reduces the levels of neuro-transmitters such as cortisol and adrenaline, whose levels increase in response to stress and, as we have seen (Chapter Three), bring about suppression of the immune system. Laughter also seems to stimulate the secretion of catecholamines which in turn release endorphins, neuro-transmitters that stimulate the pleasure centre in the brain.[13] It is well established that endorphins are the body's natural painkillers and promote feelings of well-being and relaxation. Therefore laughter may counteract the negative effects of stress and negative emotions, which are also known to trigger suppression of the immune system.

Many doctors and psychotherapists support the view of Norman Cousins, a highly influential writer who attributed his own recovery from an apparently incurable condition to the healing power of laughter.[14] Nurses also recognise that laughter makes people feel better, and humour as therapy is enjoying an upsurge of interest. This has led to the formation of the Nurses For Laughter group at Oregon Health Sciences University, the members of which wear badges with the logo 'Warning — humour may be hazardous to your illness' and wheel carts stocked with red noses and other laughter-inducing paraphernalia around their wards. Red noses also feature in the Big Apple Circus/Clown Care Unit at New York's Babies' Hospital, where clowns help children to cope psychologically with illness. A 'humour room' has been opened at St Joseph's Hospital Stehlin Foundation for Cancer Research, Houston, and St John's Hospital and Health Center in Santa Monica, California, offers patients a humour channel on closed-circuit television. In Britain laughter workshops are being promoted as part of healthcare by some regional health authorities.

The ability to see the lighter side of life is now being widely claimed as advantageous in the cure of illness, in the control of pain, and in increasing the chances of survival and improving the quality of life of those who are seriously ill. As well as being promoted for use in psychological approaches to healing and in psychotherapy, it is also finding increasing favour as an aid to stress management.

Until relatively recently, claims for the benefits of using humour in healthcare settings have not been supported by well-replicated clinical trials, but over the past ten years there has been an increasing number of investigations into its effects.[15] It is now proven that showing elderly patients humorous movies has a significant effect in relieving pain and improving mood.

However, it is as yet unclear whether brief immunological changes can exert lasting health benefits. It may be that possessing an enduring sense of humour is more important.

THE PHYSICAL EFFECTS OF LAUGHTER

Laughter does have measurable physical effects on body processes other than the immune system. A 'good' laugh exercises the muscles of the face, shoulders, diaphragm and abdomen, and more robust laughter involves the arm and leg muscles. It has been claimed that laughing 100–200 times a day is equal to about ten minutes of rowing. 'Hearty' laughter speeds up heart rate, raises blood pressure, accelerates breathing and oxygen consumption. It produces 'huffing and puffing' similar to that resulting from exercise, hence Norman Cousins reference to it as 'internal jogging'.[16] As laughter subsides, it is followed by a brief period of relaxation during which respiration and heart rate slow down, often to below normal levels, blood pressure drops and muscles relax. It isn't clear whether it is the arousal, the relaxation or both that is effective in reducing the risk of heart disease, depression and other stress-related conditions. Listening to humorous audiotapes have been found to reduce stress levels,[17] although those who gain most from comedy tapes are those who regularly rely on humour to cope, whereas anybody can use relaxation techniques to reduce stress.

A traditional Hindu meditation exercise combines both processes. Known as the 'Ha' technique, it simply requires you to focus on breathing at your stomach and to repeat the syllable 'Ha' on each out-breath. Very quickly this gives rise to a 'belly' laugh and the relaxation of conscious thought that this induces. The 'red nose' component of Exercise Three (see Chapter Two) can evoke a similar response, but as noted in the commentary, this is all too frequently suppressed by those people who fear 'looking silly', and who, for this very reason, are probably less likely to use laughter as a means of coping with stress.

Humour is just one of the ways in which you can make stress work *for* rather than *against* you by changing your response from negative to positive.

Ultimately, reducing stress is about changing your attitude so that you are friendly towards yourself, feel good about yourself and, as we shall see in the next chapter, feel good *in* yourself.

KEY POINTS

1. You may not be able to eliminate or change all your stressors but you can change your attitude to them.

2. Realising you have a choice in the matter of stress and assuming responsibility for your actions is an important step in gaining self-control.

3. Reappraising stressors as challenges and opportunities rather than as threats has a dramatic effect on the level of stress you experience and helps you to avoid the negative consequences of stress, including illness.

4. This requires you to befriend your stressors, which amounts to befriending yourself because your attitude to yourself is the major source of your stress.

5. You can befriend yourself by accepting, valuing and expressing yourself, thinking positively about yourself, indulging and asserting yourself, taking time for and amusing yourself.

6. Positive suggestions and affirmations will help you to think and feel more positively.

7. Humour and laughter are great stress-busters, with significant psychological and physical benefits.

INCREASING YOUR SELF-CONTROL

For this is the great error of our day in the treatment of the human body, that physicians first separate the soul from the body.

Plato, *The Republic*

The ancient Greeks regarded the human body as the tabernacle or temporary dwelling of the soul, mind, or *psyche* — equivalent to the 'life force' or 'breath'. For them, therefore, the soul 'breathed life' into the body and sustained it, while the body housed the soul. A similar view is found in virtually every culture, and since the earliest of times health has been viewed universally as the state of being bodily and mentally vigorous and free from disease: of having a sound mind in a sound body.

Health is not just a physical state. It embraces the whole person — body, mind and spirit. Nevertheless there is a tendency in Western culture, traceable back to its origins in early Greek civilisation, to separate the mind or soul from the body and to treat them as separate and unrelated entities. It is only during the latter part of this century that the physical effects of psychological stress have been recognised, and more recently still that the mind's role in mediating stress has been understood. However, even though this mind/body relationship is now widely acknowledged, the reverse body/mind link is not. While many people can appreciate that what is in their mind can influence what occurs in their body, they do not as easily accept that what occurs in their body affects their mind. Yet many physical stressors can be avoided once you have identified them.

DIETARY STRESSORS

You will be familiar with the idea that 'you are what you eat' but possibly not with the notion that you can be stressed because of what you eat. Yet certain foods and drinks, and various other substances you ingest, can be stressors and a constant drain on your energy. Caffeine, alcohol, tobacco, excess sugar and fats all work against the healthy functioning of your body. When we are under stress we tend to increase our intake of these substances, thereby compounding our problems and increasing the likelihood of developing stress-related illness. Under stress the body uses energy more quickly so that maintaining a healthy diet is particularly important. Yet people under stress typically under- or overeat, drink too much or too little, and by doing so place additional strain on the heart and cardiovascular system.

FOOD THAT CAN PRODUCE STRESS

Certain foods can produce a stress-like response. These are called *pseudostressors* or *sympathomimetics* because they mimic stimulation of the sympathetic nervous system — that part of the nervous system primarily involved in stress reactions. Foodstuffs and drinks containing caffeine are all pseudo-stressors. Theobromine and theophylline, found in tea together with caffeine, are also sympathomimetics. These substances produce a pseudostress response by speeding up metabolism and increasing alertness, and result in the release of stress hormones which raise heart rate and blood pressure. They also make the nervous system more reactive so that it is more likely that stressors present in the body elicit a stress response.

Caffeine

Coffee, tea, cocoa, chocolate and sweets, colas and many other soft drinks contain the drug caffeine, which stimulates the central nervous system, pancreas, heart and the cerebral cortex of the brain. Caffeine raises blood pressure temporarily and increases reactivity to stress. Consumption of it is habit-forming, and excessive intake can be damaging to the body. In laboratory animals caffeine is known to adversely affect the functioning of the nervous system. It has been speculated that its toxic effects could explain why pregnant women are often unable to tolerate coffee and tea during the first three months of pregnancy when the central nervous system of their unborn children is developing.

There is more caffeine in coffee than in tea or soft drinks. An average cup of coffee yields 90–120 milligrams of caffeine, as opposed to 40–100 mg per cup of tea and 20–50 mg per cup of cocoa or cola. Daily consumption of between two and eight cups of coffee (or, in terms of caffeine, equivalent amounts of tea or colas) provides a substantial amount of caffeine, and if this level is maintained every day it can prove dangerous to health because the body stores caffeine. A high intake of coffee is thought to increase the risk of heart disease, and its adverse effects on the stomach are well established.

The adverse effects of caffeine can be hard to identify unless you reduce or eliminate its intake. Withdrawal symptoms such as headache and nausea are common. They are usually short-lived, however, lasting from several hours to a few days. The stimulating effects of the drug can be evident after only one cup. Caffeine makes us more mentally alert and for this reason is the ally of many long-distance drivers, students and others who burn the midnight oil, but its effects wear off quickly, necessitating a further fix. In the short term it offers a quick pick-me-up which is useful for dealing with stress; thus sweet, strong tea or black coffee has become widely regarded as a panacea for all ills. However, if such drinks are used long term to combat stress, they can be counterproductive. Habitual coffee drinking is a factor in producing many stress-related disorders and psychological disturbances, including anxiety states, depression and psychosis. Tea, coffee and other caffeine-based drinks are all diuretics; that is, they increase the rate at which the body loses fluid. They exacerbate the physical effects of stress, which include dehydration and consequent thickening of the blood, undernourishment of the skin, digestive disorders and general metabolic upset. To relieve these effects, dehydration needs to be counteracted by increasing the intake of fluids in the form of water or natural, unsweetened fruit juices.

Refined Sugar and Carbohydrates

Foods containing refined sugar and refined carbohydrates such as white flour and rice are stressors, and a body already under stress has difficulty metabolising them. Refined sugar is the end product of a complex process which removes all vitamins, minerals, trace elements and natural fibre from sugar beet or cane. As a result, this type of sugar has little nutritional benefit but is high in calories or energy value. To break down sugar the body must use its B-complex vitamins. This may result in a depletion of these vitamins in the body and bring about conditions such as muscle weakness, stomach upsets, insomnia, anxiety, depression and diminished ability to produce adrenal hormones in response to stressors. Excessive sugar consumption may also lead to an imbalance in important trace minerals within the body.

The ingestion of sugar has other implications regarding stress. Consuming a large amount of sugar in a short period of time or missing meals and then ingesting sugar can result in hypoglycaemia, or low blood sugar, immediately preceded by high blood-sugar levels. This condition may be accompanied by symptoms of headache, dizziness, anxiety, trembling and irritability. Subsequent stressors are likely to provoke an unusually intense stress response. The stress response and accompanying cortisol production raise the level of glucose in the blood, which in turn puts pressure on the pancreas to maintain a normal blood-sugar level. The raised blood-sugar level in the body leads to resistance to insulin — the hormone that controls the passage of sugar from the blood to other cells in the body — and results in tiredness, depression and emotional instability. Prolonged or intense stress can exhaust the cells that produce insulin, and since these are not replaceable, the body's ability to produce insulin is compromised and diabetes may develop in genetically susceptible individuals.

Consumption of refined sugar is also linked to the development of degenerative diseases and can contribute to the development of arteriosclerosis. Foods containing refined carbohydrates do not stress the body to the same extent as those containing refined sugar, but they have been stripped of their natural fibre which is important for detoxifying the body, protecting against weight gain and the development of degenerative disease.

Fats

Eating more fats than your body needs, or consuming the wrong kind of fats, causes stress damage to the body. The consumption of too much fat prevents your body from making efficient use of carbohydrates and can encourage the development of diabetes. It raises the levels of fat, cholesterol and uric acid in the blood, which in turn contribute to the development of arthritis, arteriosclerosis and gout. A high-fat diet also contributes to premature ageing and the development of degenerative diseases. Diets high in fat and low in fibre are associated with the development of cancer, particularly of the colon.

There are two kinds of fats, saturated and unsaturated. Saturated fats occur in milk products and meat. They are high in calories, so if they feature prominently in your diet, you are likely to be overweight. Unsaturated fats are found in processed oils, margarine and many processed foods. They are chemically altered during processing and this removes essential fatty acids, which may lead to a fatty-acid deficiency even if your intake of fats is high. In a healthy diet 15–20 per cent of our daily calories should be provided by fat; but on average 45 per cent of our daily calories are in fact supplied by fat.

High levels of cholesterol are considered the major factor in the development of arteriosclerosis — the deposit of fatty plaques in our blood vessels. Our bodies produce much of the cholesterol in our blood but our diet provides the remainder. Whether or not cholesterol forms plaques in our blood vessels depends on the presence of different kinds of cholesterol-carrying proteins called lipoproteins. There are three types: low-density lipoproteins (LDL), very low-density lipoproteins (VLDL), both of which are associated with *increased* cholesterol deposits, and high-density lipoproteins (HDL), which are associated with a *decreased* likelihood of plaque build-up. The daily recommended intake of cholesterol is 300 mg, or less for people with cardiovascular disease. Foodstuffs low in cholesterol include cereals, bread, fruit, nuts and vegetables. Oils such as olive oil that consist of mono-unsaturated fats contain no cholesterol and appear to lower LDL in the blood but not HDL. You can adopt a low-cholesterol diet by eating foods containing such oils and by reducing your intake of eggs, as one egg contributes about 260 mg of cholesterol. White meat and fish are lower in cholesterol than red meat, and cholesterol intake can be further reduced by boiling, baking and steaming food rather than frying or roasting it, using low-fat dairy products and avoiding processed foods.

Processed foods

Processed convenience foods and so-called 'junk' foods are high in sugars, fats and salt. They tend to be used by people who are time-stressed and who do not take the time to eat properly or to prepare healthy meals. These foods are often very palatable and may provide comfort and pleasure when you are anxious or depressed. But if you regularly eat junk food, you are adding further stressors through your diet and thereby compounding your problems.

Processed foods often contain additives, including preservatives that lengthen their shelf life; emulsifiers that enable water and oil to mix; thickeners and stabilisers that improve and maintain their texture; and flavour enhancers that heighten their natural taste. Most are not dangerous to health although some cause stress-related allergic reactions and others are thought to be carcinogenic or cancer-producing. Some are known to be harmful, however, and controversy surrounds others, including the presence of colouring agents such as Tartrazine and Sodium Yellow — yellow colourants commonly found in soft drinks and sweets — derived from coal tar, which excites the central nervous system and has been implicated in stress-related conditions such as childhood hyperactivity, attention-deficit disorder and certain allergies.

The Effects of Stress on What We Eat

Certain substances in food, notably vitamins, can be depleted when we are under stress. The stress hormone cortisol uses up vitamins and so chronic stress can deplete vitamins in our bodies, in particular the B-complex vitamins and vitamin C. As we have seen, a deficiency in these vitamins can result in muscular weakness, stomach disorders, insomnia, anxiety and depression. Not only does stress deplete these vitamins, but since they are used in the production of adrenaline, their depletion makes us less able to respond satisfactorily to stress.

The Effects of Diet on Stress-Related Illness

Certain stress-related illnesses such as hypertension, arterio-sclerosis, cardiovascular disease, diabetes and cancer can be exacerbated by an unsuitable diet.

Diet and Hypertension

By changing your diet you can reduce your risk of developing hypertension,[1] so doctors usually advise dietary change in the prevention and treatment of this disease. Consumption of too much sodium, found in salt, can raise blood pressure in the short term by increasing fluid retention in the body, and people who consume high levels of salt tend to have high blood pressure and increased reactivity in stressful situations. A daily intake of 3,300 mg of sodium is considered safe (a teaspoon of salt contains about 2,000 mg) but on average most people in developed countries will ingest more than twice that amount, either by adding salt to foods or eating foods that contain high levels of sodium, such as processed foods, cured meats and fish, potato crisps and cereals. Most of our salt intake in fact comes from commercially produced bread. Reducing dietary sodium lowers blood pressure in both people with hypertension and those with normal levels of blood pressure.

As we have seen, caffeine can also affect blood pressure, raising it temporarily and increasing one's reactivity to stress. However, while some studies have linked higher mortality rates from coronary heart disease or stroke with high levels of caffeine consumption, lower blood-pressure levels have been found in people who regularly drink coffee. This evidence suggests that moderate daily consumption of caffeine does not appear to lead to cardiovascular disease.

Diet and Arteriosclerosis

Experts agree that maintaining high levels of cholesterol in the blood long term can lead to arteriosclerosis, heart disease and stroke and that a total serum cholesterol level of 240 mg or more constitutes a high risk. Our cholesterol levels are determined partly by heredity and partly by lifestyle. Smoking may increase LDL and lower HDL levels, but diet is clearly an important factor. Eggs, many milk products, and fatty meats contain very high concentrations of cholesterol. The higher an individual's cholesterol level in any age group, the greater the risk of developing heart disease and stroke. The risk for individuals with cholesterol levels over 245 mg is three and a half times greater than those with levels under 180 mg. Hence lowering serum cholesterol reduces the incidence of cardiovascular disease. Large reductions in serum cholesterol can be achieved with combinations of dietary and drug treatment, and in some cases arteriosclerosis can be reversed in this way.[2] However, marked reductions in cholesterol level have been associated with increases in aggression or recklessness in some individuals, leading to death from accidents, violence or suicide. So, with cholesterol, as with most other things, maintaining a balance is desirable and healthy.

Diet and Cancer

Diets low in fibre are associated with the development of cancer, especially cancer of the colon, as are the consumption of too much red meat, processed meats and bacon. Fruits and vegetables — especially when eaten raw — and high-fibre breads and cereals pose a lower risk and are recommended in the prevention and treatment of cancer. Some food substances such as vitamin A are thought to have a protective function because individuals with diets rich in this vitamin tend to have a lower risk of cancer. Many fruits and vegetables, such as tomatoes, spinach, broccoli and lettuce, and yellow/orange-coloured fruits and vegetables, such as cantaloupe melons, apricots and carrots, are rich in beta-carotene which the body converts into vitamin A.

A LOW-STRESS DIET

A low-stress diet is one that provides your body with continuous energy throughout the day, eliminates blood-sugar problems, helps you to avoid fatigue and improves your body's ability to deal with stress. Such a diet is low in fats, refined sugar and starches, and is relatively low in protein. Our bodies need amino-acids, the constituents of protein, to build muscle, produce hormones, fuel metabolism, maintain and repair cells, but if we eat too much protein we lose minerals and trace elements such as zinc, calcium, magnesium, iron and chromium from bones and tissues — minerals which are essential to our physical health and emotional well-being. Our Western diet tends to be protein-rich, and many of the traditional sources of protein — meat, fish, game and dairy products — are too concentrated a source of protein and can also be high in fat. Root crops, grains, vegetables and fruits, when comprising the major part of our diet, provide a better source of protein. It is not necessary to eat meat to stay healthy, nor is it necessarily the case that a vegetarian or vegan diet is more healthy. What is healthy is a diet with a mixed and balanced combination of protein which provides the full complement of essential amino-acids and trace elements without an excess of fat.

Consuming carbohydrates is the best means of promoting physical and emotional balance, provided these are complex carbohydrates — that is, unrefined grains, pulses, vegetables and fruits eaten in as natural a state as possible. Starches obtained from brown rice or wheat and fresh vegetables will provide you with a steady stream of energy throughout the day.

Salt intake can be reduced if you avoid processed foods, preserved meat such as luncheon meat, bacon, sausages and cured meat and fish, as well as pickles and sauerkraut. Instead of using salt, try flavouring food with garlic or herbs and spices. By eating mainly fresh foods you avoid much of the 'hidden' salt contained in processed foods, and if you're drinking enough water you will flush excess salt from your system. The key, however, is to achieve a healthy balance between levels of sodium and potassium, which means increasing your intake of potassium-rich, green, leafy vegetables, bananas and other fresh fruits. By eating what is in season you will consume the fruits and vegetables richest in nutrients at that time of year.

Water is essential for cleansing the liver and kidneys, improving digestion and as a lubricant for the joints and eyes. It clears the skin and, because stress dehydrates the body, it is good for stress-busting. Most of us normally drink insufficient water. Recommended intake is eight glasses or two and a half litres daily, and more when we are stressed, in addition to fluids normally contained in food. Try to drink the purest water possible, bottled from natural springs or, at the very least, tap water that has been filtered. It doesn't matter if it's sparkling or still, unless you find that bloating is a problem, in which case avoid carbonated water. The pitfalls of caffeine can be avoided by substituting tea, coffee and cola drinks with mineral water, natural, unsweetened fruit juice, and herbal or fruit teas.

To provide a continuous supply of energy throughout the day it is desirable to eat regularly and to avoid missing meals and the consumption of 'convenience' foods, all of which results in the lowering of blood-sugar levels. Many of these foods, such as chocolate, potato crisps or French fries, are also high in fat.

Maintaining a continuous supply of energy throughout the day can be best achieved by eating little and often. A minimum of three meals daily is recommended but six small meals are preferable at breakfast, mid-morning, lunchtime, mid-afternoon, dinnertime and mid-evening. Fresh or dried fruits, nuts, raw vegetables, low-fat yoghurt, cottage cheese and high-fibre breads are preferable to the biscuits, cake, fruit loaf, crisps, chocolate, and mayonnaise-laden sandwiches that usually comprise mid-morning, afternoon and evening snacks.

Food intake should, of course, be balanced with energetic output or work. In the morning our blood-sugar level is low following sleep. For this reason, and because historically the hardest work was done in the early part of the day, breakfast was traditionally a substantial meal. It was common for cooked meats, fish, vegetables, eggs, potatoes and cereals to be eaten at this time, and this pattern, much modified, is still evident in the cold meats, cheeses and eggs of the continental breakfast and the 'traditional' British breakfast. Even though most of us engage in less physically demanding labour than in the past, we nevertheless need fuel for our day's activities and a 'good', high-energy breakfast, which supplies our energy needs without also providing unnecessary stressors, is desirable. Whereas at night we go for anything up to twelve hours without eating, this is uncommon by day and so our energy requirements from other meals are generally less than at breakfast. Lunch is ideally a lower-energy meal than breakfast, and dinner a lower-energy meal than lunch, as by this time the energy required by work is generally much less. The wide diversification of modern-day lifestyles has led to tremendous variation in this eating pattern. Nevertheless it is perhaps true to say that for many of us this pattern is reversed. We may snatch a quick bite for breakfast or miss it out completely; work all morning so we are starving at lunchtime, when we eat a sizeable meal; sluggish in the afternoon as we digest our lunch; feel 'a bit peckish' by dinnertime, when we eat the largest meal of the day, and become inert thereafter when we slump in front of the television, before going to bed where we deposit all the energy surplus to our day's requirements as fat during sleep.

By contrast a low-stress diet which provides us with continuous and appropriate energy throughout the day is naturally low in calories and helps to prevent or eliminate a major food-related stressor — overweight.

OVERWEIGHT AND OBESITY

We add fat to our bodies because we consume more calories than our metabolism burns up. The body stores the excess calories as fat and as we get older we tend to gain weight because our metabolic rate and physical activity decline with age. To maintain younger weight levels as we get older, we need to reduce calorie intake and take more exercise. Constant dieting is a stressor because you are depriving yourself and this leads to craving. You can only lose weight effectively and maintain the weight loss by changing your lifestyle to increase your activity level, because this is the other side of the food equation. In the

US, the Metropolitan Life Insurance Medical Company has developed a chart of desirable weights based on studies of mortality rates which has become a standard for assessing overweight. You are classified as overweight if you exceed the specified range by 10–20 per cent, and obese if your weight exceeds this range by more than 20 per cent. For example, a man who is 5 ft 10 in./1.78 m (in shoes with a 1 in./2.5 cm heel) has a desirable weight range of 151–163 lb/69–74 kg, including clothing, so a man of this height weighing 180 lb/82 kg is overweight, and obese if he weighs 197 lb/89 kg or more.

There is no doubt that obesity is associated with a high level of cholesterol and the development of hypertension, coronary heart disease and diabetes, and the more obese you are, the greater your risk of developing and dying from these diseases.

Overweight and obesity can also affect your psychological well-being. Low self-esteem is associated with overweight, especially in women, not only because it is seen as unattractive but also because overweight people are often thought of as lazy and self-indulgent. Overweight children and adolescents are often teased, ostracised and bullied by their peers, which can lead to low self-confidence and self-esteem, anxiety and the development of other stress-related disorders.

What you eat and drink can not only stress your body and exacerbate stress-related illness but also reduce its capacity to deal effectively with other illnesses, as well as stressors such as drugs, adverse environmental factors and lack of exercise.

DRUGS AS STRESSORS

ALCOHOL

Like caffeine, alcohol is a socially accepted habit-forming drug. Its well-recognised health benefits include its undoubted value as a relaxant and its less certain role in reducing the incidence of heart disease. Nevertheless, like the drug digitalis, which also has a proven role in the prevention of heart disease, alcohol is a poison. Its toxic effects are clearly evident in the hundreds of babies born annually to women who drink heavily. Babies suffering from foetal alcohol syndrome are invariably undersized, underweight and show a range of impairments ranging from high levels of muscular tension to serious brain damage. In adults excess alcohol consumption can lead to strokes, cirrhosis of the liver and cancer of the throat. Alcohol also affects the brain, depressing certain areas of the cerebral cortex. This depressant effect can produce euphoria as alcohol is mildly disinhibiting, but when taken to excess over an extended period of time, it can lead to psychosis, hallucination, delirium and brain damage.

Alcohol can have a therapeutic role in relieving stress. A stiff drink can help to steady the nerves or prepare us for a demanding challenge, and in moderation alcohol can help us to relax, socialise and have fun. At a conference of the British Psychological Society in December 1996, psychologist Geoff Lowe claimed that alcohol is good for us as it makes us laugh and reduces stress levels. However, while it may help you cope with the stress of the moment, alcohol doesn't address the actual stressor, which remains when its effects have worn off. Furthermore, like coffee and tea and other caffeine-based drinks, alcohol is a diuretic and increases water loss from the body, contributing to stress in a body already dehydrated by stress. As with caffeine and other drugs, if we resort to alcohol as the sole means of dealing with stress, and if we become alcohol dependent, it is likely to become our major stressor.

In our culture, drinking is a means by which people can feel they possess power, and in a society where men are encouraged, if not obliged, to be powerful it is perceived as a macho activity. Hence feelings of powerlessness and lack of control may lead some men to drink heavily. Professor of psychology David McClelland has identified a common cycle of powerlessness that can result. Under the influence of drink men may exert power over those whom they perceive to be less powerful than themselves — usually women and children. However, the sensation of power is temporary as afterwards they often feel more out of control and have even lower self-esteem, so they resort to drink once more to bolster their feelings of power. Feelings of powerlessness in women may also contribute to their increasing use of and reliance on alcohol to help them deal with stress. However, as with men, their dependence on alcohol leads to further loss of control and increases powerlessness.

NICOTINE

Nicotine is a substance found only in tobacco. It is a complex drug that acts as a stimulant in small doses and as a depressant in large ones. Like caffeine, nicotine is also a pseudostressor. Cigarette smoking has been identified as the single most important source of preventable mortality and illness. It is estimated that an average five and a half minutes of life are lost for each cigarette smoked. Smoking increases the likelihood of coronary heart disease, respiratory problems, and lung, pancreatic and prostrate cancers. It has also been linked with susceptibility to breast cancer in women. Smokers report more chronic bronchitis and sinusitis, emphysema, peptic ulcers and arteriosclerotic heart disease than persons who have never smoked. The risk of developing or dying from smoking-related diseases is lower for pipe and cigar smokers but still considerably higher than for non-smokers.

Studies have shown that people who smoke also live unhealthily in other respects. A national survey conducted in the US found that, compared with non-smokers, smokers were more likely to drink to excess, to drive under the influence of drink, and have a less positive attitude to their health. Moderate to heavy smokers were found to lack awareness about their health and to engage more often in forms of behaviour other than smoking that increase the risk of coronary heart disease.[3] Smokers not only damage their own health but also endanger the health of others. Cigarette smoking during pregnancy is related to spontaneous abortion, premature birth, low birth weight and infant mortality. There is also evidence that exposure to a smoke-filled atmosphere, so-called 'passive smoking', increases the rate of lung cancer and heart disease among non-smokers.[4]

The reason given by most people for smoking is that has become a habit, but anxiety, nervousness, the need for stimulation and social approval underpin the development of this habit. In various studies anxiety and tension relief have emerged as significant factors in taking up and continuing smoking.[5] This appears to confirm theories of smoking which suggest that people smoke for different reasons and that these are largely determined by personality type.

According to this theory, extroverts, who tend to seek stimulation to heighten levels of arousal in the brain, smoke out of boredom in situations lacking stimulation, and also to conform to the behaviour of their peers because they are very dependent on social reinforcement. Introverts, who typically try to reduce high levels of arousal, smoke for tranquillising purposes, mostly during periods of stress. People who are anxious and emotionally unstable are prone to respond with more intense emotional reactions to environmental stress than are emotionally stable individuals. They tend to smoke a great deal in stressful situations. Irrespective of personality type, the highest rate of smoking can be expected in stressful situations.[6]

Smoking can in fact help reduce stress and help people to calm down, but only when a comparison is made with smokers deprived of nicotine — that is, those allowed to smoke only low-nicotine cigarettes. When the mood or performance of smokers who are allowed to smoke ad lib is compared with that of non-smokers, it emerges that smoking improves the mood of smokers or their performance only to the level customary for non-smokers.

Miserable people are more likely to smoke and find it harder to give up than people who are cheerful. Surveys show that more than half the people who suffer from depression smoke.

Gay Sutherland of the National Addiction Centre at London's Institute of Psychiatry observes that, whether depressed or not, people who succeed in giving up smoking for as little as a month can look forward to less stress but most of them don't stay off cigarettes long enough to realise this because in the first weeks of quitting their stress levels go up.[7]

PRESCRIBED DRUGS

Tranquillisers are widely prescribed for and used by people experiencing stress because they are relieve muscle tension and feelings of anxiety. Marketed under the generic name of Diazepam and a variety of trade names, the best known of which are Librium and Valium, tranquillisers are extensively used throughout the developed world. Valium or its analogues are taken by an estimated 10 per cent of the US population, 14 per cent of Britons and 15–17 per cent of other Europeans. The majority of users are women aged 25–34 and 45–54.

Abrupt discontinuation of tranquillisers provokes severe withdrawal symptoms, including higher levels of anxiety than that for which they were initially prescribed. This is often seen as justifying their continued usage or even increased dosage. A cycle of anxiety/dependence/anxiety is created which in itself becomes a major stressor, irrespective of any stress for which the drugs were initially prescribed. Tranquillisers are also known to have a wide range of side-effects including over-sedation, unsteadiness, drowsiness, blurred vision, loss of libido, impotence, skin rashes, urinary retention, vertigo, hypertension, jaundice, blood disorders and depression, as well as paradoxical effects such as excitement, overagitation and aggression. There can be little doubt that although widely prescribed and used in the treatment of stress, these drugs are themselves a major stressor. Taken in conjunction with alcohol, they can be very dangerous indeed.

ENVIRONMENTAL STRESSORS

Our environment, particularly the buildings in which we live and work, can be a significant stressor. This is the conclusion reached by the British Health and Safety Executive in its report on 'sick building syndrome'. The factors which most commonly go towards making a building and its occupants 'sick' are poor air-conditioning, low humidity, high levels of airborne dust and poor temperature control. These can be modified by ensuring good air flow and appropriate humidity, reducing static electricity in carpets and furnishings, dampening noise and maintaining a comfortable ambient temperature. The Health and Safety Executive report also suggests that the individual's ability to control the environment may be an important factor in maintaining good health, and recommends that workers should be allowed to adjust light levels by way of dimmer switches for overhead lighting or using table lamps wherever possible.[8]

RADIATION

Radiation emissions from visual display units and fluorescent lighting may also be significant stressors. Wherever possible it is preferable to make use of natural or non-fluorescent lighting and to observe guidelines on the operation of VDUs and other electronic equipment.

CROWDING

Limited space may be a stressor. The basic physiological effect of crowding is to increase the level of arousal (elevating blood pressure and heart rate), and while it might be pleasurable at sports and leisure events to be part of a crowd, it becomes increasingly uncomfortable in other circumstances. The important factor is not how many people occupy any given space but how an individual perceives the level of crowding. This of course varies from individual to individual and situation to situation.

NOISE

Noise is also a stressor. It can raise blood pressure and increase heart rate and muscular tension. High levels of noise are associated with cardiovascular and digestive disorders in industrial workers,[9] and noise interacts with other stress-related forms of behaviour to enhance the dangers of ill-health. In noisy conditions smokers typically increase the number of cigarettes they smoke by 15 per cent and the rate of inhalations by 30 per cent rate.[10] Noise can also effect mental health. Those of us who live or work in noisy surroundings can usually learn to screen out noise, but this doesn't necessarily mean we are not affected by it. Depending on your level of concentration and the task being performed, even low levels of noise can become bothersome. In the US, children at schools under the flight path of a major international airport were found to have significantly higher blood pressure than control children and to show some impairment when undertaking problem-solving tasks — both indicators of stress.[11]

BURN-OUT

Working conditions may be stressful for a number of reasons, whether environmental — including sick building syndrome, noise, pollution — or psychological, such as the nature of the work itself, whether there is too much or too little, whether it involves shiftwork or working in isolation, or getting to grips with masses of information or new technology. Some of us work in very stressful environments and long term these stressors can lead to burn-out — a syndrome characterised by emotional and physical exhaustion, which leads us to feel that we cannot give of ourselves psychologically; to depersonalisation, the development of negative and cynical attitudes and feelings towards those we work with; and reduced personal effectiveness, the tendency to view yourself negatively, particularly with regard to your work, to feel unhappy about yourself and dissatisfied with your accomplishments at work.

The consequences of burn-out are potentially very dangerous for the staff, clients and larger institutions in which they interact. Burn-out can lead to deterioration in the service provided by staff, speed of staff turnover, increased absenteeism and decreased morale, all of which can become further sources of stress for workers. It also correlates with various self-reported indices of personal dysfunction, including physical exhaustion, insomnia, increased use of alcohol and drugs, in addition to marital and family problems.

EXERCISE AS A STRESS-BUFFER

LACK OF EXERCISE AS A STRESSOR

As we have seen, lack of exercise is often a factor in overweight, which is a major stressor. Physical inactivity in itself can be a significant stressor. When the body is mobilised for action, the muscles become tense, the chest and throat narrow, breathing becomes shallow, levels of blood hormones, sugars and fats increase, as do heart rate, blood pressure and perspiration, while salivation and digestion slow down. These changes demand energy and, if not discharged through action, this energy remains pent up within the body, maintaining tension and imposing a considerable strain on all bodily functions and processes. If unrelieved, this will inevitably lead to breakdown and ill-health.

Exercise reduces the physical effects of stress by discharging unreleased or unexpressed energy. In so doing it reduces tension in the muscles, dilates the blood vessels, lowers blood pressure and heart rate, increases cardiovascular efficiency, aids the metabolism of carbohydrates and fats so that high levels of sugars, fats and cholesterol in the blood — associated with an increased risk of heart disease — are reduced and high-density lipoproteins, which protect against heart disease, are raised. Exercise burns calories, thereby helping to prevent hypertension, heart disease, diabetes and other conditions related to the presence of excess body fat. Regular exercise also improves the functioning of the lungs and circulatory system, tones and strengthens muscle, including heart muscle, and delays the degenerative effects of ageing. It increases energy levels and reduces susceptibility to heart attack, stroke and other stress-related diseases.

Exercise clearly has an important role in moderating the negative effects of stress, and several laboratory studies conducted in recent years have shown that physically fit people are less physiologically reactive to stress than those who are less fit.[12] Compared with women with a low level of fitness, women who are extremely fit have been found to show less increase in heart rate when subjected to a stressful psychological test.[13] Fitness also helps to lessen the adverse effects of life stress, and can protect people from illness during highly stressful periods in their lives.[14] Life stress has been shown to be strongly related to illness in people with low levels of fitness, but has little ill-effect on those people whose levels of fitness are relatively high.[15]

PHYSICAL FITNESS AND MENTAL HEALTH

It is clear that exercise plays an important role in the promotion and maintenance of physical well-being. This is not only because of the physiological benefits of exercise but also because fitness has beneficial psychological effects. If you exercise you will be more sensitive to your body and you will more readily recognise muscle tension and other signs of stress. Feelings of mastery and self-control also increase after regular exercise,[16] and this is important because the belief that you can control events has been shown to reduce reactivity to stress.[17] Typically, physical-fitness training also turns attention away from stressful circumstances in our lives.[18] It allows us to forget, albeit temporarily, the pressures and frustrations that produced our bodily tensions in the first place, and by providing a temporary respite from life stress, exercise can have a restorative function that allows us to deal with stressful circumstances more effectively.

Regular exercise also produces other psychological benefits. Fitness has been linked to improvements in mental functioning, mood states, self-image, self-confidence and general well-being. Greater mental alertness and ability can be explained in terms of increased energy and consequent reduction in fatigue. Animal studies carried out at the University of Illinois suggest that exercise increases blood flow to the brain and that this improves mental functioning. Some evidence obtained from human studies suggests that being physically fit helps people to maintain their mental ability as they age. Reasoning, breadth of vocabulary, memory and reaction time are better in physically active elderly people than in sedentary elderly people, and studies have found similar differences between physically active and sedentary young people.[19] So it seems that exercise builds up our minds as well as our bodies.

Exercise can also relieve the symptoms of depression. In one of the first major studies in this area, US physician John Greist found that exercise by itself was more effective than therapy in reducing symptoms among depressed patients. Other researchers have also shown that exercise can improve mental health. Norwegian psychiatrist Egil Martinesen has found that depression can be significantly relieved when patients exercise in addition to undergoing psychotherapy. With its focus on short-term goals, energy enhancement and step-by-step mastery of a particular activity, exercise represents the antithesis of depression, whose major symptoms include low energy, goallessness and feelings of being out of control. It can also improve the low self-esteem characteristic of people who are depressed by providing a basic sense of accomplishment, improving feelings of mastery and body image. Exercise can also provide non-threatening social support because, as John Silva, Professor of Sport Psychology at the University of North Carolina, observes, it is easy to make friendly conversation and disregard your physical appearance when you are exercising with someone else.

Body image is often of special concern to survivors of physical and sexual abuse. Exercise has proved to be especially useful in the treatment of patients recovering from such abuse because it has a positive effect on self-esteem and how they view themselves.

MINIMISING THE BODY'S STRESS RESPONSE

Exercise can also relieve symptoms of anxiety, depression and fatigue resulting from chronic tension. John Silva claims that exercise can short-circuit the cycle of mental and physical tension that characterises anxiety disorders. He points out that mental anxieties create physical tensions and that if you can dissipate these through exercise you send cues to the brain that you are less anxious. Exercise therefore provides a kind of mental 'time out' while also giving the body a break from tension.[20]

One explanation for the positive effects of exercise on mood is that it raises levels of endorphins, which produce feelings of relaxation and euphoria. However, more recent research suggests exercise increases concentrations in the brain of the hormone norepinephrine, which is thought to modulate the action of other more prevalent neuro-transmitters — such as adrenaline and cortisol — that play a direct role in the body's stress response.[21] It is not so much that more norepinephrine equals less stress and anxiety and therefore less depression, but rather that norepinephrine thwarts depression and anxiety by enhancing the body's ability to deal with stress.

The brain normally reacts to stress with a burst of norepinephrine. So sustained stress results in a depletion of norepinephrine levels in the brain. When we face a novel and challenging situation, it might be best to respond and react vigorously. Hence norepinephrine levels increase in all of us in such circumstances. However, if we are exposed to the same stressful situation repeatedly, it might be preferable to minimise the body's response each time so that it can conserve energy.

Accordingly, people who exercise regularly might be expected to be better at minimising their response to stress than those who don't.

Studies on both animals and humans have confirmed that exercise normalises the brain's stress response so that instead of reacting strongly to every situation and severely depleting the supply of norepinephrine needed to cope with the next situation, the body acts less forcibly and keeps norepinephrine levels steady. This is why people who are physically fit are less vulnerable to the adverse effects of life stress than those who are less fit.[22]

Physical fitness appears to offer some protection against stress and to serve as a stress-buffer. Biologically, exercise seems to give the body a chance to practise dealing with stress. It forces the body's physiological systems — all of which are involved in the stress response — to communicate much more closely than usual. As we become deconditioned through sedentary living, illness or injury, our bodies becomes less efficient in their ability to respond to a variety of stressors. Exercise seems to produce dynamic communication between the physiological systems of our bodies more effectively than other types of clinical intervention, and this 'workout' of the body's communication system may constitute the true value of exercise. Recognition of this has led a growing number of clinicians to use exercise in a variety of ways in their practices, especially if they exercise themselves. In addition, regular exercise may bring about more enduring change. Many people report that, having taken up exercise, they perceive situations as less stressful than formerly.

The physical and psychological benefits of exercise have prompted Jerry May, professor of psychiatry and former chair of the US Olympic Committee's Sports Psychology Committee, to assert that 'exercise is about as close to be a panacea as you can get. . . . It is a health inducer, a stress reducer and a self-confidence booster.'[23]

LOW-STRESS EXERCISE

Many people who take up exercise give up after a few attempts, usually because they overdo it. This is not surprising if they read that super-models and other media idols run up to six miles, lift weights for two hours or perform 500 sit-ups every day. However, the aim of exercise is to *de-stress* the body, not *distress* it.

Would-be exercisers typically embark on their exercise programmes with great zeal, but 'slowly does it' is the key to successful exercise. Start gently and end gradually. Beginning exercise too abruptly can cause problems with the rhythms of your heart. A 10–15-minute warm-up of gentle stretching or walking eases the body into more energetic activity and also decreases the chance of muscle strains during exercise. Stretching exercises might include: rising on your toes fifteen times in succession; forward stretches, where you hold on to a stationary object with two hands, extend your left leg behind you, bend your right knee and lean forwards, then extend your right leg, bend your left knee and so on; and knee bends, where you hold on to an immobile object with your left hand, bend your right knee, reach back and pull your foot towards your bottom with your right hand, then repeat with the left leg. A cooling-down period after exercise is also beneficial as it helps to rid muscles of lactate, a waste product of exercise, and reduces soreness in the muscles.

A common mistake made by many people who exercise is to believe that quicker and faster means better exercise. In fact slower and more gentle exercise is in many respects more beneficial than very vigorous activity. By walking briskly a fifteen-minute mile (that is, four miles an hour, or 140 steps per minute), you can burn nearly twice as many calories as you would jogging the same distance. Walking at normal pace is one of the best all-round exercises. It strengthens hips, thighs, stomach and buttocks, speeds up the metabolic rate and burns about two hundred calories every thirty minutes. Because the pace of activity is relatively slow, the body doesn't go into overdrive and draw on its carbohydrate store for energy; instead it draws energy from its fat reserves. Another great advantage of walking is that it can easily be fitted into almost everyone's life with relatively simple modifications to routine, such as walking to work — if not every day, every other day — or to the bus stop or station. Plan to walk three miles at least three times a week at a comfortable, brisk pace. Your full speed should be fast enough to make you breathe hard but not so fast that you can't talk to a companion at the same time.

The way to fitness is gradual and progressive, and it can't be rushed. Only when you can easily manage it should you increase the rate of exercise. By 'listening' to your body and becoming more sensitive to its needs, you will realise when that is. When your body tells you it's had enough or that it hurts, discontinue exercise. Don't wait until you feel thirsty before you drink water. When you feel thirsty your body is already dehydrated. If possible sip water at regular intervals when exercising to replace water lost during activity.

Exercise of relatively long duration, which uses large muscle groups and requires high levels of oxygen, is known as aerobic exercise. Aerobic activities usually involve rhythmical actions that move the body over a distance or against gravity. They include walking, jogging, skipping, cycling, long-distance swimming and fast dancing. Performed regularly with sufficient intensity and duration, such activities increase the body's ability to extract oxygen from the blood and to metabolise fatty acids and glucose efficiently. To have a beneficial effect on the cardiovascular system, 20–30 minutes of aerobic exercise is required three or four times weekly. As cardio-respiratory endurance decreases after forty-eight hours, aerobic exercise is recommended at least every other day.

UNITING BODY AND MIND

INCREASING SUPPLENESS AND FLEXIBILITY

Ideally a regular exercise programme combines activities such as walking, cycling or jogging that strengthen the cardiovascular system and those that keep you supple and flexible, such as yoga and T'ai Chi. The latter have the advantage that they combine exercise with the beneficial and relaxing effects of meditation.

Yoga

Yoga underpins the traditional medicine of India, Ayurveda. It is not merely a system of physical exercise but a complete philosophy and means of self-help that embraces the whole person in their physical, mental and spiritual aspects.

The term *yoga* derives from words meaning to 'join' or 'yoke', and it signifies the union of the individual with Ultimate Reality. It is essentially a spiritual discipline and reflects the Indian conception of health as wholeness. Indians, like other Eastern peoples, recognise the interdependence of body and mind, unlike Westerners who typically prioritise one or the other.

There are many forms of yoga but hatha yoga is most widely known and practised in the West. It is concerned with integration through strength and focuses on restoring the balance of the body and its energies through breathing and physical exercise. In so doing it removes energy blocks and chronic tension, revitalises the body and promotes relaxation. The effects of yoga have been widely studied and it is well established that regular practice reduces the negative effects of stress and brings a sense of peace, calmness and tranquillity.

T'ai Chi Chuan

Chinese culture has its own system of movement therapy, T'ai Chi Chuan — more commonly referred to simply as T'ai Chi — which, like yoga, regulates the flow of energy by conditioning the body. It is a system of gentle exercise directed to promoting the balanced flow of energy within the body and the removal of energy blocks. Daily practice is also recommended in traditional Chinese medicine as a means of preventing the illnesses resulting from tension and energy blocks, and promoting health.

The Alexander Technique

The Alexander Technique, developed by F. Matthias Alexander, shares with Eastern approaches the holistic assumption of no separation between mind and body. It also assumes that every activity, whether physical, mental or spiritual, is translated into muscular activity that becomes habitual and affects one's whole way of thinking, feeling and doing. It is not a set of exercises as such but trains the individual to become aware of how best to accomplish certain activities, with the aim of improving postural and muscular activity. In this way, not only bodily tensions and their effects can be identified and eliminated, but individuals also learn to express themselves more naturally and spontaneously. Proponents of the Alexander Technique claim that it is effective in reducing anxiety and improving mental functioning; gives rise to profound psychological and emotional changes; and induces feelings of well-being.

The Feldenkrais Method

Named after its originator, Moshe Feldenkrais, the Feldenkrais Method is similarly concerned with developing full efficiency and functioning of the body, and incorporates elements of the Alexander Technique and martial arts disciplines. It differs from the Alexander Technique in its emphasis on body motion rather than posture and as such is similar to T'ai Chi. It is in many respects similar to the system of exercise and movement developed by Rudolph Steiner — which he referred to as *curative eurythmy* — for the treatment of energy imbalance.

OTHER EASTERN THERAPIES

Eastern cultures traditionally use a variety of other practices, such as Reiki and Shiatsu (see below), to release tension and energy blocks and thereby energise and relax the body/mind complex. These practices are widely used not only as therapeutic measures to manage stress and stress-related illness but also as preventative measures designed to develop the full efficiency and functioning of the body and so avoid the need for corrective treatment.

Reiki

Reiki is a Japanese form of therapy becoming more widely known in the West. It means 'universal life energy' and was developed in the last century as a method of healing that involves the channelling and balancing of energy within the body through touch. It is gentle, non-invasive and highly relaxing.

Shiatsu

Shiatsu, which means 'finger pressure' in Japanese, is another form of therapy which uses touch and gentle pressure to remove energy blocks and tension from both the mind and the body, thereby promoting energy flow and relaxation.

RELEASING ENERGY THROUGH BODYWORK

Self-Help Approaches

Various approaches have also been developed with the common aim of relaxing the body and releasing the energy held in by various muscle groups. These therapies involve working directly on the body to unblock and regulate energy flow using massage and other forms of manipulation. Certain forms of bodywork can be self-administered, as in the case of the Japanese Do-in — which incorporates the use of pressure, friction, percussion and stretching, in addition to breathing techniques — acupressure and Shiatsu, which can be self-applied to accessible areas of the body. Reflexology, an increasing popular way of releasing energy through the use of pressure and massage, can be effectively applied just to the hands, ears and feet, which are the easiest places to treat if you practise on yourself. It is also possible to relieve tension from many parts of the body simply through massage. Aromatherapy, in which essential oils are applied through massage, is widely used as a means of stress-relief. It is highly relaxing and confers both physical and psychological benefits.

Bio-energetic Bodywork

Various kinds of more vigorous massage can also be effective in relieving tension. Many of these techniques derive from the insights of psychotherapist Wilhelm Reich who, by recognising that emotional and psychological ways of relating to the world are reflected in the body, and vice versa, laid the foundations for *psychosomatic therapy*, which in a quite literal sense addresses the psyche — the mind or soul — by way of the body.

Reichian Therapy

Reich's therapy was directed to identifying the energy blocks created and maintained by tension, which he referred to as *muscle armouring*, and eliminating them physically through deep massage. In this way, blocked *bio-energy*, as he termed it, is released at both physical and psychological levels and the natural flow of energy is re-established, normalising physical and psychological functions. He brought about the release of emotions by pressing on tense muscles in which energy is locked up, preventing physical and psychological expression. Reich focused particular attention on the muscles of breathing which he considered essential for the maintenance of an even flow of energy (for him synonymous with breath) throughout the body. He also pressed, poked, tickled and stretched muscles in a process which was invariably painful for the recipient, both physically and emotionally.

Reich's approach inspired many different forms of bodywork, known as *bio-energetic therapies*, which have the common aim of relaxing the body and releasing the energy held in by various tensions, and his insights have inspired many forms of psychotherapy.

Biosynthesis

Biosynthesis, developed by David Boadella, aims to reintegrate the major energy currents of the body — which are considered to be disrupted by stress before birth, during infancy and later life — through breath release, retoning of the muscles and postural readjustment.

Bio-energetic Analysis

Bio-energetic Analysis, developed by Alexander Lowen, also focuses on breathing, relaxing muscle tension and postural readjustment to relieve defensive blocks in the body which are thought to be established unconsciously by chronic muscle tension resulting from emotional traumas in early life and revealed in patterns of breathing.

Biodynamic Therapy

Biodynamic therapy, developed by Norwegian psychotherapist Gerda Boyeson, incorporates special deep-massage techniques to disperse the body 'armouring' by which individuals defend themselves against painful emotions. These emotions are suppressed through muscular effort and over time become such a feature of the body structure that they are no longer felt.

Structural Integration

Structural integration, also known as *Rolfing* after its originator, Ida Rolf, is a method of deep — some would claim brutal —

massage in which a therapist manipulates the body so as to return it to a desired postural and structural position, and in so doing corrects imbalances resulting from the 'armouring' process, dislodging emotional and psychic blockages. It is not simply a physical massage but a technique for freeing the body, mind and emotions from their conditioning, releasing pent-up energies and prompting insight into the fears and inhibitions which caused the blockages in the first place.

Rolfing involves loosening and lengthening specific muscles and fascia of the body, repositioning muscle fibres and returning them to their natural position. A similar technique established in America and now available in the UK is the Heller method.

Psycho-Muscular Relief Therapy

Psycho-Muscular Relief Therapy (PMRT), developed in Britain by Peter Blythe, is based on the premise that anxiety, depression and phobias are the result of people being unable to relax certain muscles that are permanently in spasm, having tightened initially to defend the individual against an intense emotional response to a specific traumatic incident or situation. Such muscular spasms are seen as a natural way of coping with life stress but which become permanent and cease to be an adaptive response, habitually transmitting via the central nervous system strong signals that the brain interprets as anxiety. PMRT aims to release the feelings locked behind muscle tension and clearly owes a debt to Reich in both theory and practice.

Ultimately each of these approaches is concerned with trying to help individuals to express themselves and thereby avoid the negative consequences of muscle tension: the stress it imposes on the body/mind complex; the resulting energy expenditure and fatigue; the inevitable wear and tear of body organs; feelings of anxiety and depression; and physical and mental illness. As such, these techniques are trying to reverse the process chronicled throughout this book, working on the body so as to relieve the stress generated by tensions initially brought about to prevent the expression of emotions that have led us into traumatic conflict with others and our environment.

Clearly none of the above approaches would be needed if we could express ourselves authentically and spontaneously all the time, without fear of the consequences. The extent to which we are able to do so determines whether we control our own lives or are controlled by others; whether we pull our own strings or, like a puppet, have them pulled for us by others. In other words, we can avoid the manipulations of others, therapeutic or otherwise, if we can learn to manipulate our own lives more successfully. As we shall see in Chapter Seven, this may require us to become aware of the subtle ways, of which ordinarily we are unconscious, in which our energies and those of other people interact.

KEY POINTS

1. Certain foods, such as refined sugar and carbohydrates, and fats; drinks containing caffeine or alcohol; and various other substances, including nicotine, food additives and tranquillisers, can be stressors and a constant drain on your energy.
2. Stress-related illnesses such as hypertension, arteriosclerosis, cardiovascular disease and diabetes can be exacerbated by your diet.
3. A low-stress diet low in fats and refined sugar, relatively low in protein and high in unrefined carbohydrates provides your body with continuous energy throughout the day, eliminates blood-sugar problems and helps to avoid fatigue. In addition, it helps to improve your body's ability to deal with stress and, because a low-stress diet is also naturally lower in calories, it also helps to prevent obesity, which can be a significant stressor.

4. Dietary stressors can reduce your ability to deal effectively with illness and stressors such as alcohol and nicotine, environmental factors and lack of exercise.

5. Exercise reduces the physical effects of stress by discharging unreleased energy. It reduces muscle tension, dilates blood vessels, lowers blood pressure and heart rate, increases cardiovascular efficiency, aids the metabolism of carbohydrates and fats, and thereby reduces susceptibility to stress-related diseases.

6. If you are physically fit, you are likely to be less reactive to stress. Exercise also directs attention away from life stress and provides a temporary respite from it.

7. Regular exercise produces other psychological benefits such as improved mental functioning, mood states, self-confidence and well-being. Regular exercise can also relieve symptoms of anxiety and depression.

8. A regular exercise programme ideally combines activities such as walking, swimming or cycling that strengthen the cardiovascular system with those that keep you flexible and supple, such as yoga, T'ai Chi, the Alexander Technique and the Feldenkrais Method.

9. Blocked energy can also be released by various bodywork approaches which involve manipulation of the body, such as massage, Reiki, Shiatsu and Rolfing.

10. The need for these physical manipulations can be avoided or reduced if you become more self-expressive and in control of yourself and your life.

HANDLING OTHER PEOPLE'S ENERGY

To be good is to be in harmony with oneself.
Discord is to be forced to be in harmony with others.
Oscar Wilde, *A Picture of Dorian Gray*

SENSITIVITY TO OTHERS

Until now we have been considering energy as though it is confined within and experienced subjectively only by ourselves. This isn't the case: not only can we detect the energy of others, but we can also be affected by it, just as they can be affected by *our* energy. As we have seen, people who are 'full' of energy seem vibrant and radiant, whereas those low in energy appear dull, dim and lacking in vigour. Abundance of energy or the lack of it affect us if we are in the company of others for any length of time: high and low spirits are definitely infectious — depressed people are as depressing to be with as lively people are invigorating. This is not simply a matter of appearances but a rather more subtle chemistry is at work. Many of us are sensitive to 'atmosphere'; we can enter a room and sense, without witnessing any obvious signs, that powerful emotions have been expressed there, or feel the emotional charge between two people. Some of us experience these sensations as a shudder or shiver, a *frisson* of fear or excitement; others describe them as 'vibrations'. We sense that some people and situations have 'good' vibrations or 'vibes', whereas others have not. We also feel that these vibrations are 'given' or transmitted to us in some way. You may dismiss these idioms as mere figures of speech but there is rather more to them. You may like to test this claim by trying the following exercise.

EXERCISE TEN

TESTING THE VIBES

Find a friend or acquaintance who is willing to act as your partner for this exercise, and ask that person to read the following instructions, or explain them to him or her yourself. Then sit opposite your partner, drawing your chairs together so that your legs are adjacent to rather than directly facing each other (see Figure 2). Ask your partner to rest his or her hands, palms upwards and open, on his/her lap, between the thighs and knees. Then extend your arms and place your hands, palms down, some two inches above the hands of your partner. Ensure that you are both sitting comfortably and can achieve this posture without straining your back, shoulders and neck. If either of you is leaning forwards even slightly, shift your chairs so that you are nearer each other and re-establish the posture. Then relax. Breathe in and out slowly, allowing your tensions to be released on each out-breath.

When you are sitting comfortably without feeling any tension, discomfort or pain in your shoulders back or neck, gradually withdraw your attention from your surroundings and direct it to your hands. Focus your attention on your hands and any sensations you experience in or around them. As you do so, close your eyes and ask your partner to do likewise. When you have done this, become aware of the energy between you. How does it feel? How do you feel? How would you describe the interaction you have with this person now, at this moment?

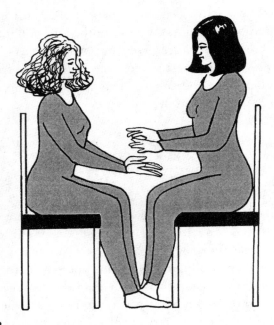

Figure 2

When you have done this, allow your energy to mingle with that of your partner. Focus your attention on the feelings and sensations you experience, imagining your energy and that of your partner in any way that comes to mind. Don't try to force the issue or to rush the exercise. Simply witness what occurs, without trying to achieve, evaluate, rationalise or censor anything. Allow yourself to experience whatever there is to experience, and give yourself several minutes in which to do so. Then imagine that you are each sending your energy into and around each other's body in any way that seems appropriate, and observing any obstructions to its movement. Make a mental note of anywhere in your partner's body that your energy seems impeded and of any other impressions that arise.

After a few minutes instruct your partner to block your energy in any way possible. Allow a minute or so to observe your feelings and reactions. Then try to overcome this barrier to your energy in any way that seems appropriate and send your energy around your partner's body, noticing your feelings, sensations and reactions as you do so. After a few minutes ask your partner to stop blocking your energy and allow it to flow again. Bring your attention to your hands once again and notice the energy there. How would you describe the energy and the interaction between you and your partner?

When you have answered these questions, repeat the exercise, this time with your partner's hands uppermost, your hands resting palms upward on your legs, and your partner 'sending' energy into and around your body. Notice your feelings, sensations and reactions as your partner sends energy into and around your body. Then notice how you block this energy, and how successfully. After a few minutes allow the energy to flow again.

When you have both completed the exercise, relax your posture and spend some time sharing with each other your experience of the exercise. Begin by reporting your experience of the transmission of energy and interaction between you, then identify any areas in your partner's body where your energy seemed impeded. When you have done this, exchange your experiences of your energy being blocked deliberately, your attempts to overcome this and your own blocking strategy. Conclude by exchanging any insights you have gained from the interaction.

REACTIONS TO THE EXERCISE

The world seems to divide quite neatly into two groups: those people who are amazed by their experiences during this exercise and those who experience nothing at all. Among the people I have worked with the former vastly outnumber the latter. Many of the former admit to being sceptical about the exercise at the outset, so their experiences are all the more significant for them. Almost without exception the people who are wholly negative about the exercise from the outset report experiencing nothing, which doesn't necessarily mean they experienced nothing, as we shall see. Interestingly, in a workshop situation where I specifically ask friends not to work together, they tend to pick partners who also report experiencing nothing, thereby reinforcing their initial negative views. Is this coincidence? I think not — for reasons I will go on to explain later.

Keeping Your Distance

Most people experience a degree of embarrassment when starting this exercise, particularly in a group situation. Selecting a partner seems to present little difficulty but sitting close to that person in the way recommended does, suggesting that we all tend to feel uncomfortable in close proximity to others, even our friends and acquaintances. Some people find the situation stressful and are clearly tense and anxious. This is usually evident in their posture, which usually appears stiff, especially around the neck and shoulders, which tend to be hunched slightly. They may sit with their chins tucked into their necks and their backs arched. Their forearms also tend to be stiff. Most commonly they have placed their chairs too far away from their partners, so their discomfort is reinforced by the strain this imposes. Some are reluctant to reduce their discomfort by drawing closer to their partner. When I explain that unless they do so they will find it difficult to continue with the exercise, they reluctantly draw closer, and almost immediately become more relaxed simply because the unnecessary tension they have imposed by trying to keep their distance is removed.

Whether or not we are aware of it, we are all trying to keep our distance from others and this imposes some degree of tension and strain on us. Psychologists have identified a 'critical distance' we strive to maintain around ourselves. If this is breached, we feel threatened and react by either withdrawing ourselves, pulling back sharply from those who have invaded our personal space, or aggressively hitting out at them, shoving them away, or telling them in no uncertain terms to keep off.

These 'flight' or 'fight' reactions are characteristic of the stress response, and a clear indication that invasions of our personal space are an important stressor. For this reason where proximity is unavoidable, such as in elevators and commuter trains, we defuse the situation by avoiding eye contact with our oppressors, staring at the floor or into empty space; anywhere other than directly at them. This is because interpersonal gaze is another potential stressor. A hard stare or glare is generally perceived as a warning, as aggressive — so much so that we can only tolerate very brief eye contact with people who are non-intimates before we feel threatened by them and our stress reactions are triggered. This is why as young children we learn that it is rude to stare and are actively discouraged from doing so. Those people who did not heed this early instruction tend to find that they become ostracised for their anti-social behaviour and are shunned.

Gaze reveals that our energy is not confined to our bodies but extends much beyond and can affect others at a considerable distance. Indeed all our senses and many of our faculties extend far beyond the confines of our body, carrying our energy with them, and if you doubt this, consider for a moment the effect on a group of squaddies of the drill sergeant-major's voice.

In the above exercise eye contact is avoided by the seating position of the participants and also by them closing their eyes, but nevertheless the proximity required is very threatening to some people and can provide insight into a major source of their stress.

Once seated with their eyes closed, most people find they can begin to relax. Others find it almost impossible. This may be because their mind tapes begin to operate, telling them that it is irregular to relate to others in this way and that proximity of this kind is unacceptable. They may be concerned about their own bodily smells and sounds, or other aspects of themselves that they may reveal at close quarters. These messages are probably the basis for much of the interpersonal stress, tension and anxiety in their lives.

Handling Interpersonal Energy

Most people find that they experience various sensations when focusing on their hands. There may be tingling, or a prickly 'pins and needles' sensation, a tremor or vibration, or even the sensation of a mild electric shock. Most commonly there is a feeling of great warmth. Even people who say they have experienced nothing during the exercise usually admit that they have felt this heat. Many of them have dismissed it as 'only' body heat, even though the heat may be intense rather than merely warm as skin usually is to the touch. Many people can distinguish the direction of this energy, as streaming either from themselves into their partners or vice versa — or both.

Where a high intensity of warmth is perceived by both parties, they usually report that there is positive energy and a good connection between them. Sometimes one partner may feel heat emanating from his/her hands but sense a coldness coming from the other person, like a draught or breeze that is repelling their hands. These chilly, cool, frigid sensations usually lead one or other person to describe the relationship he/she has with the other in these terms.

Similarly the relationship between the two persons may be described in terms of the 'spiky' or 'prickly' sensations experienced by one, other or both of them. Such feelings are perceived as dismissive, if not hostile, and those who project them may admit, when confronted with them, that they find intimate interactions with others difficult. It may or may not be their intention to keep others at arm's length, and for those who do not consciously choose to repel attempts at intimacy, feedback of this kind from others can be very beneficial, particularly if it enables them to begin to understand how they are achieving this effect. Those people who do wish to keep people at arm's length are usually aware that they signal this to others in some way, but may not be aware how they do so. Nevertheless my observation that 'like attracts like' — that people who don't want to open themselves to others tend to be drawn to work together — suggests that this attitude can be detected. I believe this is an example of resonance — the sympathetic vibration of energies sharing a similar frequency, or, in other words, the attraction we have for other energy forms vibrating at a similar rate to ourselves.

The attraction I have observed in workshop participants is of two kinds — between individuals who are closed energy systems on the one hand, and between more open ones on the other. In the former, neither party is open to the other and so they remain closed off from each other and experience nothing, thereby reinforcing their initial attitude that there is nothing to be gained from such an exercise. More open people are also attracted to each other. Generally they are able to relax and allow their energies to mingle, and report a pleasant, close, warm feeling and a sense of intimacy, even with strangers.

Visualising Energy and Energy Blocks

Most people are surprised to find that they can imagine their energy moving through the body of their partner in various ways. They may imagine it in the form of light, dazzling arrows, fluid of some kind, colour, air, regiments of soldiers — the invention is endless; and they can usually sense areas of their partner's body where the energy seems to be impeded. When they report this to their partner afterwards, they often find that their impressions tend to correspond with the location of long-standing physical problems or injuries. That this should be so invariably astonishes both parties, but it is unsurprising when you realise that we block the flow of energies within ourselves through muscle tension and that chronic muscle tension in areas where we habitually block energy leads to pain, inflammation, wear and tear of body parts and organs, muscular strains and sprains, and increased susceptibility to injury and damage. Very commonly the energy blockages are in the head region, and people thus affected will often report that they suffer from headache or migraine, but they may occur anywhere in the body and correspond with disease or discomfort in that area.

Marilyn was quite puzzled to find that her partner, Joan, appeared only to block the flow of her energy in one of her feet and was shocked when Joan told her that she suffered from an ingrowing toenail on that foot which caused her constant pain. Marilyn is not alone in being amazed to discover that through this exercise she could detect a physical problem in her partner, but in fact this is precisely how many healers detect problems in their clients — by sensing their energy blocks. In this instance, the sensing device is our imagination, but it is also possible to sense this energy directly. You may find it interesting to try the following exercise.

EXERCISE ELEVEN

GETTING IN TOUCH WITH OTHERS

Ask your partner to stand up and close his or her eyes. With your hands about two inches from the surface of your partner's body, start to explore its outline (see Figure 3). Begin at the head and slowly move your hands up around the head, then down to the neck and shoulders without touching them and remaining silent as you do so. Focus your attention on your hands and fingers and on any feelings or sensations you experience in or around them. Proceed slowly downwards, moving your hands from around the shoulders to the upper body, front and back, over the stomach and hips and down the legs, paying careful attention to any change of sensation in your hands and fingers.

Having completed your exploration, go over the entire body again — back, front and sides — from head to toes. Then change places with your partner so that he/she may explore the outline of your body in the same way. When you have both finished, share with each other your impressions of what each of you experienced during this interaction.

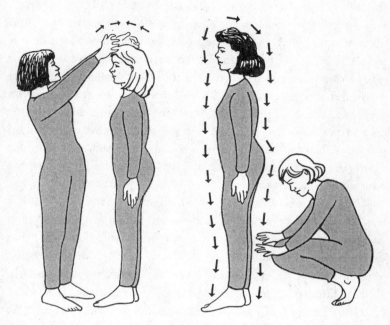

Figure 3

REACTIONS TO THE EXERCISE

You may have found that you experienced heat and similar tingling sensations in your hands to those you felt in Exercise Ten. You may also have noted variations in temperature or vibration in certain places, or sensed 'holes' or empty spaces. When discussing these experiences with your partner, you will probably find that these sensations relate to areas of the body where there is pain, injury or other problems. Typically, areas of pain feel hot and tingly, and areas where energy is blocked feel cold. Areas where energy is not flowing as a result of blockages tend to feel empty or as though a cool breeze is blowing through them.

What you are sensing is the energy field around the body and the patterns of movement within it. You may be sceptical that this is so, but there is now little doubt that the body emits a radiant energy which relates specifically to the location and intensity of energy within it and reveals something about how it is functioning. Throughout history there have been seers or clairvoyants who have been able to see this energy field, and many more who have sensed it and been able to act upon what they sense for healing purposes. Indeed knowledge of this energy field is the basis of traditional Chinese and Indian medicine. Now even orthodox Western physicians also diagnose illness in this way, and one such practitioner, John Pierrakos, has conducted extensive research into the phenomenon.

While this energy field is self-evident to many healers, it is less so to most of us. Nevertheless, we are all sensitive to it in varying degrees, although we may not be consciously aware that we are. The human energy field has also eluded scientific detection until recently. Only since the 1960s have sufficiently sophisticated devices been developed for measuring the subtle electromagnetic emission of energy in and around the body. As a result, there is now an increasing interest in analysis of the relationship between the body and its energy field for use in the diagnosis and treatment of illness.

Therapeutic Touch

Dolores Krieger, formerly a professor of nursing in the US, developed and pioneered the technique known as Therapeutic Touch, which is now widely taught and practised as a professional nursing skill throughout North America, and has recently been introduced to Britain. Therapeutic Touch is based on the principle that healing is the rebalancing of energies within the energy field of the body and the belief that these can be sensed, redirected and rebalanced by passing one's hands through the energy field surrounding an individual. Differences in energy flow resulting from imbalance and disease are detected through sensations in the hands, in the form of variations in temperature, tingling or pins and needles, or a sensation of pulsing pressure or minor electric shock. Bound-up or congested energy is then released by making stroking or sweeping gestures away from the affected part of the body, and this is often sufficient to relieve any symptoms of disease and mobilise the subject's energy. The healer may also place his or her hands on either side of the affected area and imagine directing energy into. He or she would then visualise the transmission of energy to other parts of the body, to cool or sedate, warm or stimulate these areas until the whole body 'feels' the same all over, with no perceptible differences in any part.

Numerous studies have shown the effectiveness of Therapeutic Touch, which has been demonstrated to bring about a significant reduction in patient anxiety, clinical symptoms and pain.[1]

You can practise Therapeutic Touch by learning to centre yourself physically and psychologically — that is, by relaxing and focusing your attention inwards so that you effectively maintain a meditative state throughout the procedure described above. Indeed Therapeutic Touch may properly be regarded as a process of healing meditation or visualisation.

Resisting Contact with Others

When you are on the receiving end of energy transmitted by your partner in Exercises Ten and/or Eleven, you may be able to sense that energy. Your imagination may transform it in various ways so that you imagine it as light or colour, or taking a particular shape or form, and you may also detect the areas of your own body where the flow of this energy is impeded. You may find that you imagine these blocks in certain ways, as a vice perhaps, or a portcullis; traffic lights or a filter. You may gain further insight into these blocking devices from the part of Exercise Ten which asks you to block the flow of energy entering your body. Many people are surprised at how suddenly images leap into their mind of drawbridges being raised, iron doors descending, barricades being erected, waters rising against the intrusive energy. Most people imagine blocking the energy in their hands, wrists or forearms but may also do so at other points in their body.

This blocking action is invariably accompanied by a very dramatic increase in tension in these areas. You probably noticed an increase in the tension in your forearms, temples, forehead, jaw, neck and chest. You may have found yourself clenching your teeth tightly and possibly pulling your chin in towards your neck as you tried to repel your partner's energy. These are all indications of the ways in which you defend yourself against the unwanted intrusion of other people's energy. If you experienced tension, pain, discomfort or other symptoms in these parts of your body, it is likely that they result from this resistance. You may be totally unaware that you have been resisting others, so it is worth reflecting on this part of the exercise and asking yourself if and in what other circumstances you experience similar sensations in your body. If you can identify situations in which these sensations occur, try also to analyse what it is in those situations that you are resisting. Are certain people and activities literally a pain?

Mollie admitted that her daughter is. Every time she visits, Mollie experiences chest pains, which she had not previously associated with keeping her true feelings 'close to her chest' before performing this exercise. Ted reckons his wife gives him plenty of 'earache' by her continual nagging. He hadn't realised that he 'turned a deaf ear' to her much of the time by actually turning his head away from her, and that the resulting tension in his head and neck caused his frequent headaches. Meanwhile Doreen's 'headache' is the interminable weekly staff meeting which bores her 'stiff', and Jean's 'pain in the neck' is her line manager at work. David responded to a colleague's constant whinging by gritting his teeth to keep in the 'biting' remarks he felt like saying, and Gordon 'shrugged off' his overbearing boss with perpetually hunched shoulders. People and situations that irritate us but which we cannot avoid represent stressors, and our responses to them often produce the facial tics and tremors, the stiff upper lips, chips on the shoulder and pained expressions that characterise most of us. Constant or frequent exposure to such stressors or to a combination of them can drain our energy, leaving us listless.

In the workplace we typically confront many different people and forms of activity, and resisting the inroads some of them make into our lives can be exhausting. This is particularly difficult if you work in an open-plan office. Lack of privacy, too much noise and too many distractions can lead to stress. This was the finding of a study by Dr Phillip Leather of Nottingham University, who found that within three months of moving from private offices to open-plan environments most employees develop stress-related symptoms such as headaches, and lose enthusiasm for their work.[2]

The people we live with can be equally or more demanding of our energies. Children require boundaries to be set for them or otherwise they will encroach on others. Establishing these boundaries is one of the major functions of parenting, but many parents don't do so effectively, with the result that their children constantly make demands on them and others, which may become intolerable. Children whose parents never established boundaries for them will grow into adolescents and adults who encroach on others, invade their privacy and personal space, fail to respect their rights or property, and never realise when they have gone too far. Dealing with them can tax our energies to the full.

Some people drain the energies of those around them like 'psychic vampires'. For many years, Fiona attributed the fatigue she experienced when visiting the home of her parents-in-law to the central heating. She no sooner entered the house than she began yawning, deeply and frequently, something she never did elsewhere, and it became a source of embarrassment to her as at times she found it difficult to remain awake. The first time she travelled in a car with her mother-in-law, she also began yawning, so much so that she had to open the window in order to stay awake. This incident made her realise that it was not the central heating that drained her energy but her mother-in-law herself — a very demanding woman who always had to be the centre of attention and deferred to constantly.

Overcoming the Resistance of Others to Us

Handling others involves more than resisting their unwanted attentions, impositions, demands and requirements. We also have to overcome their resistance to us. As Exercise Ten reveals, some people are not open to the overtures of others. They simply 'don't want to know' and defend themselves, albeit unconsciously, against such overtures. We usually find that we 'can't get through' to such people, however hard we try — and the effort involved in trying takes its toll our energy. Our difficulty may be in getting our point of view, or maybe our feelings, across to another. We may believe we are at fault because we don't appear to be able to 'reach' certain people or influence them in any way, or because they take no notice of us. If we have low self-esteem, this apparent rejection may lead us to feel badly about ourselves, to feel a failure. Befriending, influencing, being liked by or winning the respect of such people may become a big issue for us. It may grow out of all proportion and become an obsession. We may feel that we have to win over a particular person 'at all costs', and the costs can be staggering because, while all our energy is invested in this endeavour, it is no longer available to us for meeting the demands of everyday living. Trying to impress ourselves on others uses energy, as Exercise Ten reveals, and in the long term its effects can be debilitating.

When you tried to overcome the energy blocks imposed by your partner, how did you react? Did you imagine the block in a particular way, and if so did it influence your response? If you imagined the block as a steel door descending, you may have responded by imagining your energy as a battering ram or rocket-powered missile. These images reveal much about the respective power of you both. Clearly a guillotine-action, solid steel door several feet thick is a very effective barrier and if you imagine your energy as shafts of sunlight, you may not be able to penetrate it. On the other hand, if you are lightning quick, you may be able to enter before the door descends, or if you imagine your energy as a nuclear warhead, the door may offer no defence whatever. You may sense that you can overcome or undermine your partner's barrier, or simply wear it down. You may realise that your partner is a 'pushover' and that no great force is needed to overcome his or her resistance. It may be, however, that you found yourself engaged in an equal struggle with your partner and this part of the exercise became a battle of wills.

Ultimately your responses are matters of attitude and self-belief — the conviction that you *will* impose your energy on another, irrespective of what opposes it. And your partner may sense this strength of character or forcefulness and give way before it. Irrespective of how we construe it, some of us know already or realise in this exercise that we can direct our energy at will and overcome obstacles, while others know this not to be the case and that they can be easily overwhelmed. Some of us may be surprised to discover we are more or less forceful than we believe ourselves to be.

Irrespective of your attitude to the task, it is important to notice how you attempt to overcome the barriers imposed by your partner. Many people find that they become tense in their forearms, but most people experience an increase of tension in their head, jaw and chest, and especially in their solar plexus and the belly area just below their navel. The latter region is known to the Japanese as the *hara* and is considered the centre of force within the body. Controlling the *hara* is essential in martial arts' practices, in which the aim is to use your opponent's energies to overcome him, while concentrating your own energies in the *hara*, thereby rendering yourself invincible.

If you find the sensations in this area and the solar plexus very familiar, you need to ask yourself how much of your energy goes into trying to overcome other people's opposition and resistance. If you suffer pain, discomfort and other symptoms in these areas, it may indicate that your attempts to impress or impose yourself on others are a major source of stress and tension, for them as much as for you, and could result in illness. Stomach upsets, disorders of the gut and genito-urinary tract may result from the stress imposed by constant or frequent tension in these areas. If you can identify these problems, you need to ask yourself whether you are striving to overcome resistance generated by your own aggressiveness or intrusiveness. Do others defend themselves against you because you try to meet your needs at the expense of theirs? Do you pose a threat to their self-esteem? Do you tend to exploit others if you sense they are less forceful than you?

Poor Resistance

During Exercise Ten you may have realised that your attempt to block the energy of your partner was unsuccessful. You may have felt yourself give way to your partner and imagined how this occurred. Some people find themselves taken off guard because they don't defend themselves swiftly enough, or because they dither about how best to do so. Others find their defences are inadequate for the task. You may simply have given up trying. If you sensed or imagined that your resistance was weak, you may realise that this was not an isolated occurrence and that it is a more general quality of your character or being. On the other hand, you may be surprised that this was so because you normally think of yourself as someone able to stand up to others; or as someone who doesn't give up easily. You may wonder how your partner affected you as he or she did, and how you can change yourself so as to deal with other people's energies more effectively and not be so influenced by them.

BEING AUTHENTIC

In every encounter each individual has potential influence on others. To understand who influences whom and how, we need to consider the principle of magnetism. In physical terms, a magnet is a metallic substance whose inner structure is characteristically organised so that all the atoms have their magnetic moments aligned in the same direction, as a result of which it attracts and magnetises other metals. A magnet does not *perform* magnetism, but *is* magnetic; the very nature of its being effects changes in other substances. It is influential as a result of its internal organisation or harmony of composition. Unified field theory and quantum physics both hold that the more integrated and unified a physical field, the more force it exerts. This would seem to be no less true for human beings as for other physical objects.

A major principle of Carl Rogers's theory of personality and the practice of his Person-Centred Therapy is that the greater the degree of harmony within an individual, the greater is his or her ability to influence or affect others. He coined the term *congruence* to describe the condition where there is harmony between what a person *is* at any point in time and what he *appears* to be. It is the opposite of presenting a façade or defensive front and is equivalent to expressing authenticity, because a person who is truly or genuinely him- or herself is not compromised and has no inner division between this true self and a false one. So, an authentic person is essentially someone who is unified or 'together' — a balanced individual whose various parts are in harmony or agreement. Such a person is not divided internally by the competing demands and interests of true and false selves, and does not confuse the different needs and requirements of each. As a result, his or her true self is not compromised by others. The energy of such a person is focused rather than diffused, and available for use in the present. Such a person is, like a magnet, effective, and will *be* influential.

There is little doubt that in any interaction between two persons, some influence will occur, however unconscious or unintentional, where one person is more congruent and the other less so. The greater the discrepancy between them in respect of congruence, the greater the degree of influence will be. Congruence exerts powerful interpersonal influence and is also responsible for the charisma, forcefulness or sheer power of certain individuals. We may find them irresistible. Conversely, incongruence produces weak and unimpressive individuals, who are easily led or influenced by others, and prone to fall apart or break down under stress because their energy is dissipated. If and when this occurs, they are typically told by others to 'pull themselves together' and to 'get a grip' on themselves and their lives. This advice is sound because such people are unhealthy in the literal sense of not being whole, unified or 'together', and they can become healthy, whole or together only by taking up the threads of their lives and beginning to pull these strings themselves rather than allowing them to be pulled by others. So, if you want to make friends and influence people, and avoid the tension created by their unwanted influence over you, you need to master the art of pulling your own strings. You need to make stress a positive force in your life, working *for* you rather than against you.

KEY POINTS

1. Your energy is not confined within your body but extends beyond it and affects others, just as you are affected by *their* energy.

2. You are sensitive to the energies of others even though you may not be aware that you are.

3. You use much of your energy dealing with the energy of

others both at home and at work; resisting unwanted energy and trying to overcome the resistance of others to you.

4. You resist others by blocking their energy. You achieve this through muscle tension and this can lead to wear and tear of parts of the body, to pain and other physical symptoms of dis-ease.

5. You can become more aware of your energy blocks and can also develop your sensitivity to the energy of others through visualisation.

6. You can learn how to relieve energy blocks and to rebalance the energies of others by Therapeutic Touch.

7. You are more susceptible to the influence of others if your energy is less focused and organised than theirs.

8. You can become more effective and influence others if you are congruent or authentic; if your true self and the self you project to others are consistent.

9. You can become more congruent by healing any divisions within yourself.

10. You can achieve this by taking control of your life; identifying and acting on your own needs, wishes and desires rather than exclusively those of other people; that is — by pulling your own strings.

LET GO OF YOUR HANG-UPS

If you are feeling strung up or strung out, you may be able to gain immediate relief in the following ways:

Get it off your chest Scream, cry, laugh or bang the table — in the privacy of your own room, office or car. In this way you will release the emotions generating the stress you are feeling.

Distract yourself Thinking about something else or taking exercise will distract attention from your stressors and prevent you dwelling on them and becoming locked into a cycle of worry.

See the funny side of your situation Don't take yourself or others so seriously. Humour will help you gain a different perspective on issues and a sense of control.

Be broad-minded As George Eliot observed: 'It is a narrow mind which cannot look at a subject from various points of view.'

Think positively Look on the bright side. Remember Walt Whitman's advice: 'Keep your face always towards the sunshine and the shadows will fall behind you.'

Use affirmations Reinforce positive thinking with positive messages. Tell yourself 'this is easy' rather than 'this is impossible'; 'I am coping' rather than 'I can't cope'; 'There is a vacant parking space waiting for me' rather than 'I'll never find anywhere to park'. Use affirmations when you exercise by mentally rehearsing them when relaxing between activities.

Stretch yourself Have a good stretch to release tension from your muscles and relax them.

Count to ten Mentally scan your body from your toes to the tip of your chin while counting to ten, releasing the tightness in various parts of your body as you do so. At the count of one, release the tightness in your toes, feet and lower legs; at two, release the tightness in your knees; at three, release the tightness in your thighs; at four, release the tightness in your buttocks and thighs; at five, release the tightness in your lower back; at six, release the tightness in your stomach; at seven, release the tightness in your arms and hands; at eight, release the tightness in your shoulders and neck; at nine, release the tightness in your facial muscles; and at ten, release the tightness in your jaw. Note any areas of residual tension and work on them for a few moments by tightening and letting go of them.

Open your mouth It is impossible to be fully relaxed with a clenched jaw so simply relaxing the jaw by opening your mouth will help you to relax and reduce any tension and pain in the head and neck area.

Use imagery as an aid to relaxation Imagine gripping a gold coin so tightly you can feel the effects of this action throughout your body, and then let go; imagine resisting a rising floor with the outstretched fingers of your hands until it falls away from under them; imagine you are a puppet being pulled upwards by strings attached to your head, arms and shoulders and that the strings are then cut so that you fall limply like a rag doll. Imagine your tensions as areas of ice being melted by a warm sun and flowing out of your body, leaving you feeling pleasantly warm and heavy.

Breathe your tensions away Breathe deeply, from the stomach, allowing your stomach to expand as you inhale and contract as you exhale.

Use imagery to assist deep breathing Imagine breathing coloured light in through your nose; visualise it circulating through your head, down your spine, and upwards towards your mouth, pushing your tension ahead of it in the form of fog.

Monitor your tension When you have identified the muscles most likely to retain tension, learn to scan these for tension at regular intervals — such as during news bulletins on the radio or during television advertisements; when bells ring at the end of work shifts or classes; or when waiting in queues, at checkouts or traffic lights — and relax these muscles by alternately tightening them and then letting go.

Massage tight muscles to release the tension held there.

Use pressure With your fingertips press on your temples. This relaxes muscles of the head and jaw. Applying pressure to other points, such as the back of the neck and between the eyebrows, can also relieve tension and pain.

Take a break Relax by visualising yourself on an empty beach on a warm, sunny day, or in some other place where you can feel really relaxed and at ease. Allow yourself to spend a few minutes there enjoying the sights, sounds, smells and sensations.

Take a shower This will help relieve stress not only by soothing tense muscles but also because water droplets enhance the quality of the air you breathe. Beware, however, of taking a cold shower or a cold swim because these can have an adverse effect on the cardiovascular and respiratory systems and circulation. Plunging an arm into cold water can provoke the characteristic symptoms of coronary arterial disease in angina sufferers, so avoid cold dips unless you are certain you are free from heart disease.

Take a hot bath Hot water, by contrast, helps to reverse the stress response by restoring a normal rate of circulation and enabling the body to relax.

Wash your hands free of tension Even simply washing your hands under running water will help you to release tension.

Use oil Add relaxing essential oils to the bath to soothe your mind as well as your body: peppermint, sandalwood and rosemary for mental fatigue; jasmine, rose or patchouli for physical exhaustion; and lavender for promoting relaxation, calmness and sleep.

Take time out After your shower or bath, lie down for a few minutes and listen to music, a relaxation tape, or simply enjoy the silence.

Take a walk Exercise will help you work off tension, and a change of scenery will alter your perspective and help take your mind off your stressors. Walking in open spaces will also help you get away from the effects of 'sick' buildings and other environmental stressors.

Walk the dog Better still, stroke your dog — or cat. Stroking pet animals is relaxing and is a proven way of reducing or reversing the adverse physiological effects of stress.

All of these methods will help you to defuse some of the stress-related flashpoints of your life. However, if you want to achieve lasting relief from stress, you need to take and maintain control of your life.

GET A GRIP ON YOURSELF

Take the first step Begin by expressing yourself. As the saying goes: 'A journey of a thousand miles begins with one step' — so start in small ways to assert your needs and act on them.

Take back your power Don't give your power away to others by constantly seeking their confirmation, endorsement, validation and approval of your thoughts, feelings, actions, beliefs and opinions. The only approval you need is your own. Be your own judge of what is appropriate for your needs.

Develop muscle sense Become aware of the tensions in your body, and the situations in which they arise, by focusing your attention on them. Relax these tensions in whatever way is most congenial to you. Be aware of the feelings that are released as you do so; try to express them rather than bottle them up.

Take note of your lifescript Identify the messages you relay to yourself — the *shoulds* and *should nots*, the *oughts* and *musts* you live by — and decide which of these are relevant to *your* life and chosen by *you*. Begin to eliminate the messages that are irrelevant to you and to replace them with messages that relate to *your* needs, wants, aims, objectives and values. Decide what really matters to you, what is essential in your life, and discard what is trivial and inessential. Carefully scrutinise e-motive messages — those that motivate you — to determine whether they are appropriate to your needs. Heed Dr Bernie Seigel's advice: 'Don't climb the ladder of success only to find when you reach the top that it is against the wrong wall.' Establish what is right for you, and pursue it. You can't please everyone so you might as well please yourself. Learn to listen to yourself and act on your own, self-generated wisdom rather than the received wisdom of others.

Make up your own mind Don't allow others to dictate to you. Become more single-minded through meditation, self-hypnosis, relaxation methods, Autogenic Training, creative visualisation and guided imagery.

Take time for yourself Learn to value yourself and your time. Make time for yourself, your family and friends. Take time for yourself and the activities you wish to pursue. Take holidays — make time to relax.

Take a stance Learn to say 'no' to unacceptable demands and to act on this without feeling guilty. Learn to delegate.

Take stock Eliminate unnecessary stressors — directives, instructions, rules, codes of conduct, standards, expectations that weigh heavily on you — and lighten the burden you carry through life.

Take a new look at your life Change your attitude to the stressors you cannot eliminate. Remember that how you react to situations is determined by how you perceive them. Life, with all its ups and downs, is like a roller coaster. You can ride the roller coaster fearfully, with gritted teeth and closed eyes, longing for it to stop so that the torture will be over; laugh and enjoy the thrills and spills; or simply take it in your stride. Whichever way you respond, it is still the same ride, but by changing your attitude and the way you view the situation, you can change the way you react to and experience it. Think positively instead of negatively. By doing so you will appraise the situation differently, as a challenge or adventure rather than a form of torture. By thinking positively you will change your feelings towards the situation, feeling excitement and enthusiasm rather than terror and dread. As the saying goes: 'When in deep water, become a diver.'

Make friends with yourself Change your attitude to yourself. Instead of being your own worst enemy, become your best friend. Think positively about yourself. Forgive yourself; see your 'failures' as opportunities to learn, grow and develop.

Take care of yourself Eat a balanced diet. Don't burden yourself with unhealthy or processed foods, excess sugar, fat, salt, caffeine, nicotine or alcohol. Eat foods that are seasonal and in as natural a state as possible. Drink at least eight glasses of water each day. Strive for moderation or balance in all things, including exercise.

Take opportunities Don't live with regrets. Tell yourself that for every door that closes another opens. Live in the present. Stop using today's energy to keep the past alive. Take a tip from the Queen of Hearts:

'The horror of that moment,' the King went on, 'I shall never, never forget.'

'You will, though,' the Queen said, 'if you don't make a memorandum of it.'

(Lewis Carroll, *Alice Through the Looking Glass*)

Take it easy Don't be such a hard task master. Allow yourself to have fun — tell yourself regularly and often that you deserve to.

Get real Express yourself honestly so the true or real you is apparent at all times and there is no inconsistency or incongruence between how you know yourself to be and how you seem to others.

Pull yourself together Strive to achieve and maintain a state of inner harmony or accord, with no incongruity between any part or parts of yourself. Become healthy and whole.

Live life wholly, and to the full In the words of Oscar Wilde: 'Don't squander the gold of your days listening to the tedious, trying to improve the hopeless failure, or giving away your life to the ignorant, the common and the vulgar. These are the sickly aims, the false ideals of our age. Live! Live the wonderful life that is in you.'

ENERGY QUESTIONNAIRE

PART I

Carefully read the statements below and rate yourself for each one on a score of 0–5.

Score:
0 if this statement applies to you every day
1 if it applies several times a week
2 if it applies once a week
3 if it applies a few times a month
4 if it applies once a month or less
5 if it never applies to you.

Enter your score for each statement in the space provided. Then, when you have entered a score for each one, add these together to obtain a total score.

Score	Statement
1.	I feel tired when I wake up and have to face another day.
2.	I feel physically exhausted.
3.	I feel depressed.
4.	I feel tense and anxious.

5. . . . . I feel tired doing almost nothing.
6. . . . . I feel emotionally drained.
7. . . . . I feel under pressure.
8. . . . . I feel that everything I do is an effort.
9. . . . . I feel run down and unwell.
10. . . . . I feel that I can't get on with my work

Total Score. . . . . . .

PART II

Now read the following statements (see below) and rate yourself for each one on a score of 0–5.

Score:
0 if this statement never applies to you
1 if it applies once a month or less
2 if it applies a few times a month
3 if it applies once a week
4 if it applies several times a week
5 if it applies every day.

Enter your score for each statement in the space provided. Then, when you have entered a score for each one, add these together to obtain a total score.

Score   **Statement**
1. . . . . I feel full of energy.
2. . . . . I feel in high spirits.
3. . . . . I feel on top of the world.
4. . . . . I feel enthusiastic and keen to get on with my work.
5. . . . . I wake up refreshed and enthusiastic about the day ahead.
6. . . . . I feel I do things easily.
7. . . . . I feel I don't tire easily.

8. . . . . I feel calm and relaxed.
9. . . . . I feel physically fit and healthy.
10. . . . . I feel I can cope with anything.

Total Score. . . . . . .

Now add the total scores of Parts I and II to give a grand total, and insert this in the space below.

Grand Total Score. . . . .

HOW TO INTERPRET YOUR SCORE

- If you scored between 0 and 10, you are almost certainly ill, or feeling unwell most of the time. You probably find it difficult to get up in the morning and are fatigued all the time. You may feel that you haven't enough energy to drag yourself around, and find just about everything in life an effort. You may find that despite your tiredness you have difficulty sleeping. You are physically tense at all times and cannot relax, and you tend to be anxious and/or guilty. Probably you spend a good deal of time thinking about your past or your future and give little of no attention to the present. It may seem that you have too much on your mind to be able to do so.

- If you scored between 20 and 30 (which is roughly equivalent to 0–3 on the simple rating scale in Chapter One), your energy levels are dangerously low. You probably feel physically and emotionally drained much of the time and may suffer from stress-related ill-health. You don't express yourself or your needs. Indeed, you probably have no clear idea of what your needs are, and have no time to meet them even if you do. You tend to be on the go all the time trying to meet the needs and demands of others, and may be finding it difficult to keep going. Other people may see you as energetic because of this and may not recognise how low you feel. You may resent this but do not feel that you can express this to others. You know you need to relax, but probably don't know how to and would feel guilty if you attempted to.

- If your overall energy is in the range 40–70 (roughly equivalent to 4–7 on the simple scale given in Chapter One), you may feel below par much of the time and tired for no apparent reason. You may also be susceptible to infections, viruses, colds and flu, as well as tension headaches, migraine, stomach upsets and general aches and pains. You probably realise that you need to relax more but feel that there isn't enough time in the day for all the things you have to do, so you are constantly under pressure.

- If your overall score is 50, you may find that your energy level fluctuates for no apparent reason — that you feel better on some days, in some circumstances and with some people than others, although you may not be sure why.

- If your overall score is between 70 and 90, you may feel that while you would benefit from the occasional pick-me-up, you are generally fairly energetic, healthy and able to enjoy life. You are usually resistant to infections, viruses, colds and flu and recover quickly from injury. Your outlook is generally positive — you try to make the best of things, and you are able to focus your energies so that you accomplish a gool deal. You manage your time well, take breaks and holidays and make time for yourself, family, friends and others. You are able to relax and enjoy yourself, to express and have confidence in yourself.

- If your overall score is 100, you are a forceful individual. You may intimidate others with your boundless energy and zest for life. You are in peak condition, full of energy, positive in outlook and with a sense of well-being. You organise your time well and live life to the full, with minimum stress.

Indeed, what others find stressful you regard as positive stimulus or challenge. You have high resistance to illness. Your energies are focused in the present; you don't dwell on the past and are not anxious about the future. You sleep well, and although you work and play equally hard, you generally find life easy, highly rewarding and fulfilling.

ENDNOTES

CHAPTER ONE

1. G. V. Prosser et al., 'Exercise after myocardial infarction: long-term rehabilitation effects', *Journal of Psychosomatic Research* 29/5 (1985), 535–40.
2. A. Maslow, *Towards a Psychology of Being*, 2nd ed., New York: Van Nostrand 1968.
3. Ibid.
4. C. B. Bahnson, 'Emotional and personality characteristics of cancer patients' in A. Sutnick, ed., *Oncological Medicine*, New York: University Park Press 1975.
5. A. Bandura, 'Self-efficiency: towards a unifying theory of behavioural change', *Psychological Review* 84 (1977), 191–215; L. G. Calhoun, T. Cheney and A. S. Dawes, 'Locus of control, self-reported depression and perceived causes of depression', *Journal of Consulting and Clinical Psychology* 4/42 (1974), 735; K. A. Wallston and B. S. Wallston, 'Who is responsible for your health?' in G. Sanders and J. Suls, eds, *The Social Psychology of Health and Illness*, Hillsdale, New Jersey: Erlbaum 1982, 160–70; M. Watson, S. Greer, J. Pruyn, B. van den Borne, 'Locus of control and adjustment to cancer', *Psychological Reports* 66 (1990), 39–48.
6. F. S. Perls, *The Gestalt Approach and Eye Witness to Therapy*, New York: Bantam 1976.

CHAPTER TWO

1. See also H. Graham, *Healing with Colour*, Dublin: Gill & MacMillan 1996.
2. W. Reich, *The Function of the Orgasm*, tr. T. P. Wolfe, New York: Orgone Institute Press 1942.

CHAPTER THREE

1. M. Friedman and R. H. Rosenman, *Type A Behaviour and Your Heart*, New York: Alfred A. Knopf 1974.
2. M. Williamson, *A Return to Love*, New York: Thorsons 1992.
3. For more information on visualisation and other self-help techniques see H. Graham, *Visualisation: An Introductory Guide*, London: Piatkus Books 1996, and *The Magic Shop: An Imaginative Guide to Self-Healing*, London: Rider 1992.

CHAPTER FOUR

1. Reuters Business Information, *Dying for Information? An investigation into the effects of information overload in the UK and worldwide*, 1996.
2. M. Marrin, *Daily Mail*, 17 October 1996.
3. Carlos Castaneda, *A Separate Reality*, Harmondsworth: Penguin Books 1973.
4. D. A. Throll, 'Transcendental meditation and progressive relaxation: their psychological effects', *Journal of Clinical Psychology* 37 (1981), 776–81.
5. J. Stoyva and T. Budzynski, 'Cultivated low arousal — an anti-stress response?' in L. V. Dicara, ed., *Recent Advances in Limbic and Autonomic Nervous System Research*, New York: Plenum 1973.
6. P. B. Fenwick, S. Donaldson and L. Gillis, 'Metabolic and EEG changes during transcendental meditation', *Biological Psychology* 5 (1977), 101–18; R. K. Wallace and H. Benson, 'The physiology of meditation' in C. T. Tart, ed., *Altered States of Awareness: Readings from Scientific American*, San Francisco: W. H. Freeman and Co. 1972.

7. J. A. Stern et al., 'A comparison of hypnosis, acupuncture, morphine, Valium, aspirin and placebo in the management of experimentally induced pain', *Annals* (New York Academy of Science) 296 (1977), 175–93.

8. H. B. Benson with M. Z. Zlipper, *The Relaxation Response*, London: Collins 1975.

9. Cited in Swami Deva Wadud, *Osho. Meditation: The First and Last Freedom. A Practical Guide to Meditation*, Cologne: Rebel Publishing House 1992, 16–17.

10. K. Pelletier, *Mind as Healer, Mind as Slayer*, London: George Allen & Unwin 1978, 252.

11. T. E. Lawrence, *The Seven Pillars of Wisdom*, 1926.

CHAPTER FIVE

1. C. Dodwell cited in S. Melchett, *Passionate Quests: Five Modern Women Travellers*, 1991.

2. W. Shakespeare, *Hamlet*, II. ii. 249.

3. S. C. Kobasa, S. Maddi and S. Kahn, 'Hardiness and health: a prospective study', *Journal of Personality and Social Psychology* 42 (1982), 168–77.

4. J. H. Schultz and W. Luthe, *Autogenic Training: A Psychophysiological Approach to Psychotherapy*, New York: Grune & Stratton 1959.

5. C. R. Kelly, 'Psychological factors in myopia', Proceedings of the American Psychological Association, 31 August 1961; J. H. Lewis and T. R. Sarbin, 'Studies in psychosomatics', *Psychosomatic Medicine* 5 (1943), 125.

6. Reported in *Medicine Now*, BBC Radio 4, 14 October 1988.

7. H. Graham, *Time, Energy and the Psychology of Healing*, London: Jessica Kingsley 1990, 96–107.

8. S. Freud, *Jokes and Their Relation to the Unconscious*, New York: W. W. Norton & Co. 1960.

9. J. Thurber citing Lord Boothby in J. Levine, 'Humor as a form of therapy' in A. J. Chapman and H. C. Foot, eds, *It's a Funny Thing, Humor*, Oxford: Pergamon 1977, 127–39.

10. Cited in Swami Deva Wadud, *Osho. Meditation*, xii.

11. N. Chogyam, 'Laughing possible!', *Caduceus* 9 (1990), 14–16.

12. Cited in S. Silverman, 'Commentary by Samuel Silverman', *Integrative Psychiatry* 3/2 (June 1985), 114.

13. B. Saper, 'Humor in psychiatric healing', *Psychiatric Quarterly* 59/4 (Winter 1988), 306–19.

14. N. Cousins, *Anatomy of an Illness as Perceived by the Patient: Reflections on Healing and Regeneration*, New York: Bantam, 1981.

15. E. R. Adams and F. A. McGuire, 'Is laughter the best medicine?', *Activities, Adaptation and Ageing* 8/3–4 (1986), 157–75; B. Saper, 'Humor in psychiatric healing'.

16. N. Cousins, *Anatomy of an Illness*.

17. K. M. Dillon et al., 'Positive emotional states and enhancement of the immune system', *International Journal of Psychiatric Medicine* 15 (1985), 13–17.

CHAPTER SIX

1. L. Stamler et al., 'Primary prevention of hypertension by nutritional-hygienic means: final report of a randomized controlled trial', *Journal of American Medical Association* 262 (1989), 1801–7.

2. D. H. Blankenhorn et al., 'Beneficial effects of combined colestipol-niacin therapy on coronary atherosclerosis and coronary venous bypass grafts', *Journal of American Medical Association* 257 (1986), 3233–40.

3. J. M. Remington et al., 'Current Smoking Trends in the United States: the 1981–1983 Behavioural Risk Factor Surveys', *Journal of the American Medical Association* 253 (1985), 2975–8.

4. J. M. McGinnis, D. Shopland and C. Brown, 'Tobacco and health: trends in smoking and smokeless tobacco consumption in the United States', *Annual Review of Public Health* 8 (1987), 441–67.

5. C. D. Speilberger, 'Psychological determinants of smoking

behaviour' in L. D. Tollison, ed., *Smoking and Society*, Lexington, MA: Heath 1986, 89–132.

6. H. J. Eysenck, *The Causes and Effects of Smoking* London: Temple South 1980, and *Smoking, Health and Personality*, New York: Basic Books 1965.

7. For the research referred to in this and the preceding paragraph see S. Schachter, 'Pharmacological and psychological determinants of smoking', *Annuals of Internal Medicine* 88 (1978), 104–14.

8. J. Oliphant, 'Sick Building Syndrome?', *Occupational Safety and Health* 25 (1995), 14–15.

9. P. A. Bell, J. D. Fisher, A. Baum and T. C. Greene, *Environmental Psychology*, 3rd ed., Fort Worth, Texas: Holt, Rinehart & Winston 1990.

10. R. D. Cherek, 'Effect of acute exposure to increased noise levels of background industrial noise on cigarette smoking behaviour', *International Archives of Occupational and Environmental Health* 56 (1985), 23–30.

11. S. Cohen, G. W. Evans, D. S. Krantz and D. Stokols, 'Psychological, motivational and cognitive effects of aircraft noise on children', *American Psychologist* 35 (1980), 231–43.

12. S. Keller and P. Seraganian, 'Physical fitness level and autonomic reactivity to stress', *Journal of Psychosomatic Research* 28 (1984), 279–87; K. C. Light et al., 'Cardiovascular responses to stress II. Relationships to aerobic exercise patterns', *Psychophysiology* 24 (1987), 79–86; D. Sinyor et al., 'Experimental manipulation of aerobic fitness and the response to psychosocial stress: heart rate and self-report measures', *Psychosomatic Medicine* 48 (1986), 324–37.

13. D. S. Holmes and D. L. Roth, 'Association of aerobic fitness with pulse rate and subjective responses to psychological stress', *Psychophysiology* 22 (1985), 525–9.

14. Ibid.; J. D. Brown and M. Lawton, '1986 Stress and well-being in adolescence: the moderating role of physical exercise', *Journal of Human Stress* 12 (1986), 125–31.

15. J. D. Brown, 'Staying fit and staying well: physical fitness as a moderator of life stress', *Journal of Personality and Social Psychology* 60/4 (1991), 555–61; J. D. Brown and J. M. Siegel, 'Exercise as a buffer of life stress: a prospective study of adolescent health', *Health Psychology* 7 (1988), 341–53.

16. A. D. Simons et al., 'Exercise as a treatment for depression: an update', *Clinical Psychology Review* 5 (1985), 553–68.

17. J. Rodin, 'Aging and health: effects of the sense of control', *Science* 232 (1986), 1271–6.

18. M. S. Bahrke and W. P. Morgan, 'Anxiety reduction following exercise and meditation', *Cognitive Therapy and Research* 2 (1978), 323–33.

19. For the studies mentioned in this paragraph see B. Azar, 'Exercise fuels the brain's stress buffers', *Monitor* (July 1986), 18.

20. For the studies mentioned in this and the preceding two paragraphs see T. DeAngelis, 'Exercise gives a lift to psychotherapy', *Monitor* (July 1996), 24.

21. B. Azar, 'Exercise fuels the brain's stress buffers'.

22. Ibid.

23. T. DeAngelis, 'Exercise gives a lift to psychotherapy'.

CHAPTER SEVEN

1. P. Heidt, 'The effect of Therapeutic Touch on the anxiety level of hospitalised patients', *Nursing Research* 30/1 (1981), 32–7; J. Quinn, 'Therapeutic Touch as energy exchange', *Advances in Nursing Science* (January 1984), 42–9; P. Turton, 'Healing: Therapeutic Touch' in D. F. Rankin-Box, ed., *Complementary Health Therapies: A Guide for Nurses and the Caring Professions*, London: Croom Helm 1988, 148–62.

2. Study reported at the Occupational Psychology Conference, Blackpool, January 1997.

INDEX